ADULT ADHD SURVIVAL TOOLS

EMPOWERING STRATEGIES TO MANAGE TIME, MAINTAIN PERSONAL AND PROFESSIONAL RELATIONSHIPS, RESOLVE WORKPLACE CHALLENGES, AND USE DAILY DECISION-MAKING FRAMEWORKS

REESE HUNTER

CONTENTS

INTRODUCTION

You might grapple with a whirlwind of thoughts and tasks every morning, feeling like you're perpetually behind and struggling to catch up. It isn't just about having a rough start to the day. It's a constant, exhaustive battle that seems to engulf every aspect of life. It is a glimpse into the dynamic, often chaotic life of someone living with Adult ADHD. But amidst this chaos, there's also a potential for unique creativity and vibrancy — a side of ADHD that doesn't always make the headlines.

I know this firsthand. My loved ones' and friends' journey with ADHD, diagnosed and undiagnosed, has been a rollercoaster of challenges and revelations. From feeling overwhelmed by day-to-day tasks to struggling with maintaining relationships and meeting workplace expectations, I've lived through their struggles with the spectrum of difficulties that come with this condition. However, through years of searching for help through experience and research, I've found effective strategies and tools that have transformed lives, and I'm passionate about sharing these with you.

This book can be your comprehensive survival guide. It will empower you with strategies to manage your time, strengthen your personal and professional relationships, navigate workplace challenges, and create effective decision-making frameworks. I aim to provide you with a toolkit that addresses the hurdles and leverages the strengths inherent in living with ADHD.

What sets this book apart is its foundation in the latest research and its integration of cutting-edge technology and apps tailored explicitly for managing ADHD. It is not just another book on the subject. It is a lifeline crafted with the latest advancements to make your journey less chaotic and more successful.

Whether you are a young adult stepping into the complexities of life, a professional striving to balance productivity, or anyone in between, this book speaks to you. It is crafted for men and women alike, addressing the unique challenges and opportunities of managing ADHD at various stages of life.

I want you to feel like you're receiving advice from a friend who deeply understands this condition's nuances. This book celebrates your potential and focuses on turning ADHD traits into assets, empowering you to lead a fulfilling life. These tools can be of benefit even if you have not been "officially" diagnosed with ADHD traits.

Moreover, this book emphasizes a communal experience. It shares personal stories and insights from diverse individuals with ADHD, fostering a sense of belonging and understanding. It is about building a community where shared experiences and proven strategies pave the way for collective empowerment.

Rest assured, scientific research and proven practices explicitly tailored for ADHD support every piece of advice in this book. This commitment to evidence-based information ensures you receive reliable guidance every step of the way.

I invite you to join me on this transformative journey. With an open mind and a readiness to try new approaches, you'll discover that you can navigate the complexities of ADHD with newfound confidence and resilience. Let's embark on this path together, learning and growing with each page turned.

The following chapters will delve into each aspect of managing ADHD—from organizing your daily life to thriving in your personal and professional spaces. Get ready to explore a range of tools and strategies that will equip you to handle the demands of ADHD with expertise and optimism.

MASTERING TIME MANAGEMENT

Have you ever felt like you're in a constant race against the clock, trying to squeeze every task into your day, only to end up feeling like you've barely made a dent in your to-do list? If this scene sounds all too familiar, you're not alone. Many adults with ADHD experience these time management challenges daily. Time management isn't just about keeping appointments or staying on schedule; it's about finding peace amidst the chaos, gaining control over your day, and, ultimately, freeing up time to enjoy the aspects of life that truly matter to you.

Time management for those with ADHD can often seem like a puzzle where the pieces don't quite fit. Traditional methods don't always cater to the unique challenges presented by ADHD, such as variable attention spans, impulsivity, and the tendency to underestimate or overestimate the time needed for tasks. But here's the good news: this chapter tackles transforming your relationship with time. It's not just about managing time; it's about mastering it in a way that respects your neurodiversity and leverages your strengths.

1.1 TAILORING TIME BLOCKING FOR ADHD

Understanding Time Blocking

Time blocking is a dynamic time management method that involves dividing your day into blocks of time, each dedicated to accomplishing a specific task or group of tasks. This method is particularly beneficial for individuals with ADHD for several reasons.

- Firstly, it helps reduce decision fatigue — a common issue where making too many choices drains mental energy.
- By planning how your hours will be spent, you remove the need to decide what to do next, allowing you to conserve energy for task execution.
- Moreover, time blocking enhances focus by providing clear guidelines on what you're supposed to be doing and when. This guide can be beneficial if your attention tends to wander.

Customizing Time Blocks

The key to successful time blocking when you have ADHD is customization. Standard time blocks may not align with your attention span, which can vary significantly from one individual to another.

- Start by identifying the length of time you can work effectively before taking a break.
- For many with ADHD, shorter periods — perhaps 25 minutes, followed by a 5-minute break — work well, a technique popularized by the Pomodoro Method.

- However, you might operate better with 45-minute blocks or even hour-long stretches.
- Experiment with different durations to find what best suits your natural rhythm.
- Remember, consistency is less about uniformity and more about what consistently works for you.

Incorporating Flexibility

ADHD can often mean unexpected shifts in focus or sudden new priorities cropping up throughout the day. Hence, flexibility in time blocking is crucial.

- While having a structure is important, build in some open blocks with nothing scheduled.
- These open blocks act as buffers to accommodate tasks that might take longer than expected or to manage unexpected issues.
- They reduce the stress of running behind schedule, which can exacerbate feelings of anxiety and overwhelm.

Visual Time Block Schedules

To make your time-blocking plan clear and easily accessible, utilize visual tools.

- Digital calendars are excellent as they can be updated quickly and synced across all your devices.
- Color-coding these calendars can further enhance this strategy. For example, use blue for work tasks, green for personal errands, and red for important deadlines.
- A physical planner with color-coded sections can serve the

same purpose for those who prefer something more tangible.

- The key is visibility. Your time blocks should be somewhere you can see them easily and frequently throughout the day, helping to keep you on track and aligned with your day's structure.

Time management is more than just a set of strategies; it's a fundamental component of living well with ADHD. By tailoring these techniques to fit your unique needs, you're setting yourself up for a productive day and a fulfilling life. As you explore the nuances of each method and find what combinations work best for you, remember that this is about creating a system that respects your individuality and embraces your strengths.

1.2 TAILORING TIME MANAGEMENT TOOLS FOR ADHD

When it comes to managing time effectively, especially for those with ADHD traits, the traditional one-size-fits-all tools often fall short of meeting your unique needs.

- The standard planners, apps, and schedules do not accommodate fluctuating focus and energy levels.
- However, with some customization, these tools can become invaluable allies in the daily struggle to manage time better.
- Let's explore how these conventional tools can be adapted to better suit the ADHD mind, ensuring they enhance productivity rather than add to frustrations.

Traditional time management tools often lack the flexibility and visual elements crucial for someone with ADHD.

- For instance, a standard planner might not provide enough space for notes or reminders that can be crucial for remembering tasks when dealing with ADHD.
- Consider customizing these tools using color-coded systems in your planners or digital apps.
- Color-coding can visually separate different tasks — work, personal, urgent, etc. — making it easier to assess your day or week at a glance quickly.
- Additionally, many digital apps allow you to set repetitive reminders.
- These can be a game-changer for keeping track of recurring tasks without wasting mental energy trying to remember them.

Choosing the right tools is more about understanding what complements your individual ADHD symptoms and less about what is trending.

- For instance, a planner that allows for diagramming or drawing alongside traditional scheduling might be ideal for visual thinkers.
- On the other hand, if you process information better auditorily, setting up voice-activated reminders or choosing apps that provide auditory feedback could be more beneficial.
- The goal is to match the tool to your strengths and how your ADHD manifests, which can significantly boost your efficiency and reduce the stress of managing time.

Integrating these tools into your daily life seamlessly is crucial for sustained success.

- Begin by placing these tools where they are easily accessible.
- If you use a digital tool, install and sync it on all your devices.
- This way, whether you use your phone or tablet or sit at your computer, your schedule and reminders are up-to-date and visible.
- For physical tools like planners, keep them open on your desk, carry them in your bag, or have a designated spot at home where you can easily access them.
- It's also helpful to build a habit of checking these tools.
- For example, you could review your digital calendar every morning while drinking coffee or glance over your planner every night before bed.
- Consistency in when and how you use your tools reinforces their presence in your life, making it more likely that they'll be helpful.

Lastly, the effectiveness of any tool isn't set in stone. Regular assessments of how well your chosen tools work for you are necessary. What works today might not be as effective next month or next year as your responsibilities and environments change.

Every few weeks, evaluate whether your tools still serve their purpose.

- Are they helping you manage your time better?
- Are you still using them consistently?

  - If not, try to understand why — is it the tool itself, or has something in your routine changed?
  - Do you need to adjust, such as switching from a digital to a physical planner or vice versa, changing the types of

reminders you use, or even changing the time of day you engage with your tools?

- This feedback and adjustment cycle ensures that your time management strategy evolves with you and continues to meet your changing needs.

By customizing your time management tools, choosing ones that align with your cognitive style, integrating them fully into your routine, and regularly updating your strategy, you create a dynamic system that not only accommodates your ADHD but also capitalizes on your unique skills and preferences. This tailored approach makes day-to-day life less stressful and enhances your ability to achieve more with less effort.

1.3 OVERCOMING TIME BLINDNESS WITH VISUAL AIDS

Time blindness is a common but often misunderstood aspect of ADHD. It refers to the difficulty in accurately perceiving and estimating the passage of time, which can significantly impact one's ability to manage daily tasks and long-term projects. For someone with ADHD, an hour can feel like minutes when hyperfocused or like seconds are dragging into hours when tasks are unengaging. This skewed perception often leads to procrastination, missed deadlines, and constantly feeling rushed or behind schedule. Understanding and mitigating time blindness can radically improve productivity and well-being.

One effective strategy to combat time blindness is using clocks, timers, and countdown apps.

- Placing large, easily readable clocks throughout your living and workspace ensures that time is always in your peripheral vision, constantly reminding you.
- Setting digital timers or countdown apps on your phone or computer to remind you of the start or end of time blocks can help. For example, if you decide to work on a task for 30 minutes, setting a timer for this duration can help anchor your perception of time to reality, preventing you from overextending into a hyperfocus trap or switching tasks too soon.

Setting alarms for transitions between activities is another crucial tactic.

- These alarms can act as endpoints for current tasks and cues to start new ones.
- Setting these alarms a few minutes before the transition is beneficial. A buffer period provides time to prepare mentally for the switch.
- This method helps manage the day's structure more effectively, ensuring you know the time and use it purposefully.
- For instance, if you have a meeting at 2:00 p.m., setting an alarm at 1:50 p.m. can give you a 10-minute window to wrap up whatever you're working on and shift your focus to preparing for the meeting.

Creating time awareness routines throughout the day can further enhance your time perception.

- These routines could be as simple as checking the time every hour or aligning time checks with regular daily activities, such as after meals or breaks.
- This habit improves time awareness and helps better structure the day by breaking it into smaller, manageable segments.
- Over time, these regular checks can help recalibrate your internal clock, making time management more intuitive.

Additionally, creating a sensory-rich environment can significantly help with time management. Integrating visual and auditory cues can cater to sensory preferences, ensuring effective reminders.

- Visual tools can be helpful, like sticky notes with time-specific tasks or digital displays that change color as time passes.
- Auditory cues, such as chimes or alarms with different tones for different tasks, can complement these visual reminders.
- For instance, a gentle chime might signify a reminder to take a break, while a more urgent alarm could indicate an approaching deadline.

Using these strategies, you transform your environment into a space that supports your time management efforts. These adjustments make the concept of time more tangible and less abstract, accommodating the unique challenges posed by ADHD and paving the way for a more organized and less stressful day.

1.4 PRIORITIZATION TECHNIQUES THAT WORK WITH AN ADHD MIND

Prioritization can often feel like a high-stakes puzzle for those with ADHD. The challenge isn't just about deciding how to accomplish everything; it's about distinguishing what needs immediate attention from what can wait. It can be especially tricky when every task seems equally urgent, or your focus shifts rapidly among various demands. However, mastering prioritization can significantly ease daily pressures, creating a more manageable and less overwhelming schedule. Let's delve into some ADHD-friendly techniques that can help you prioritize effectively, making your day smoother and more productive.

Identifying Priorities

One of the first steps in effective time management is learning to distinguish between urgent and important tasks. This distinction might not always be clear, especially when your ADHD brain urges you to tackle everything at once.

- Urgent tasks require immediate attention, leading to significant consequences if not addressed promptly.
- Important tasks, on the other hand, do not require immediate attention but are crucial for long-term goals and well-being.
- A simple yet effective way to categorize these tasks is using a two-by-two matrix known as the Eisenhower Matrix (See Exhibit 1). This matrix allows you to visually sort your tasks into four categories: urgent and important, important but not urgent, urgent but not important, and neither urgent nor important.

- This visual categorization simplifies decision-making and clarifies your day's or week's priorities, ensuring you're attending to what truly matters.

The "Must, Should, Could" Strategy

The "Must, Should, Could" strategy can be particularly beneficial for further refining your prioritization skills.

This method involves breaking down your tasks into three categories:

- '**Must do**,' which includes tasks that are essential for your day or week;
- '**Should do**,' which consists of tasks that are important but not critical; and
- '**Could do**' consists of tasks that would be nice to complete but aren't urgent.
- Start by listing all the tasks you think you need to do, then categorize them into these three groups.
- Classifying your tasks helps reduce anxiety by making your to-do list more manageable and ensuring that you focus on the most impactful activities. It's about making intentional choices about where your energy should go, which can be a game changer in managing ADHD-related decision fatigue.

Using Technology

In our digital age, numerous apps and tools can assist with task prioritization, many of which are particularly useful for those with ADHD.

- For example, apps like **Trello** or **Asana** allow you to visually organize tasks into boards and lists, which can be categorized using the "**Must, Should, Could**" strategy or the Eisenhower Matrix method.
- These tools often feature reminders, due dates, and the ability to share your lists with others, which can help keep you accountable.
- Many apps are also customizable, allowing you to set up notifications that work best for your attention span and working style.
- For instance, you can adjust the settings to receive fewer alerts if continuous reminders are distracting.
- The key is to choose apps that sync across all devices, ensuring that your priorities are clear and accessible whether you're on your phone, tablet, or computer.

Daily Prioritization Practice

Finally, developing a daily prioritization practice can significantly enhance your ability to manage tasks effectively.

- Each morning, take a few minutes to determine the day's top priorities. Writing these down in a planner or inputting them into a digital app is helpful.
- As the day progresses, be flexible in adjusting your priorities based on new information or shifts in your schedule — common occurrences in the life of someone with ADHD.
- This practice helps embed prioritization into your daily routine and improves your ability to distinguish between varying levels of urgency and importance over time.
- Remember, the goal of prioritization isn't to get everything done. Instead, it's to focus on what is most important,

reducing stress and increasing your satisfaction with your day's accomplishments.

1.5 SETTING REALISTIC DEADLINES AND MEETING THEM

When it comes to managing deadlines, the often unpredictable nature of ADHD can turn what should be a straightforward task into an uphill battle. Recognizing ADHD traits, it's crucial to approach deadlines with strategies that acknowledge and accommodate ADHD-related challenges. By modifying the traditional SMART goals framework and introducing specific techniques tailored for ADHD, you can transform how you handle deadlines from a source of stress to a manageable — and even rewarding — part of your daily life.

SMART Goals for ADHD

Traditionally, SMART goals are **S**pecific, **M**easurable, **A**chievable, **R**elevant, and **T**ime-bound. However, for those with ADHD, a few tweaks to this model can make goal-setting more effective.

- Let's consider 'Achievable' in the context of ADHD to mean setting realistic goals given your unique fluctuations in focus and energy.
- Flexibility is also key. Rigid deadlines can often lead to a sense of failure if unexpected ADHD symptoms disrupt your plans. Therefore, adapting the 'Time-bound' component to be more flexible — allowing for extensions or adjustments based on your day-to-day condition — can reduce anxiety and increase your chances of success.
- For instance, if you aim to complete a project, you might set a target week instead of a fixed deadline. This target gives

you the wiggle room to accommodate good and bad ADHD days, making your goals more attainable and less daunting.

Buffer Time for Distractions

Incorporating buffer times into your deadlines can be a game-changer. ADHD can often bring with it a host of distractions or a sudden loss of focus, which can derail your progress on tasks.

- By proactively adding extra time to your original estimates — an additional 15 minutes to wrap up a task or an extra day for a larger project — you give yourself the grace to handle interruptions without the panic of falling behind.
- This buffer not only caters to ADHD's inherent unpredictability but also eases the cognitive load of constantly recalibrating your schedule.

Using Timers for Deadlines

Timers are not just tools to remind you when time is up. They can also be a potent means of creating a sense of urgency that helps maintain focus.

- For many with ADHD, the pressure of a ticking clock can enhance concentration, making it easier to stay on task until completion.
- You can use timers to break down work into manageable intervals, known as timeboxing, where each box is a particular task or part of a task.
- This method keeps you on track and provides regular check-ins on your progress, which can be incredibly satisfying and motivating.

Accountability Strategies

Meeting deadlines can sometimes require a village, especially when ADHD is in the mix.

- Setting up accountability systems, such as regular check-ins with a peer, mentor, or coach, can significantly bolster your commitment to your goals.
- These check-ins provide an opportunity to review progress, troubleshoot issues, and adjust plans as necessary.
- Moreover, knowing that someone else is aware of your deadlines and is rooting for your success can be a powerful motivator.
- It transforms the often solitary task of meeting deadlines into a collaborative effort where support is readily available when needed.

Celebrate Small Wins

Finally, the power of positive reinforcement cannot be overstated, particularly for those with ADHD, who often face repeated challenges and setbacks.

- Celebrating the completion of tasks — no matter how small — can boost your self-esteem and reinforce productive behaviors.
- Set up a reward system for yourself. For example, treat yourself to a coffee after completing a small task or plan a night out for larger project milestones.
- These celebrations make the process more enjoyable and help forge positive associations with meeting deadlines,

gradually easing the dread that might typically accompany them.

By rethinking how you set and meet deadlines through these ADHD-friendly strategies, you create a framework that supports rather than stifles your productivity. This approach not only acknowledges the challenges posed by ADHD but also highlights the potential for adaptability and success, providing a robust foundation for managing time and tasks effectively.

1.6 MANAGING PROCRASTINATION THROUGH MICRO-TASKING

Procrastination is an everyday companion for many, but for those with ADHD, it can be a particularly stubborn foe.

- It isn't just about laziness or poor time management; the roots of procrastination in ADHD are profoundly psychological and intertwined with the brain's wiring.
- Individuals with ADHD often struggle with executive function challenges, which can impair their ability to prioritize, start, and complete tasks.
- ADHD issues with impulse control and inconsistent attention compound procrastination tendencies. These ADHD traits might make a task seem too daunting or monotonous, pushing one to avoid it altogether.

Understanding this, we can approach procrastination not as a character flaw but as a symptom requiring management.

- One effective technique in this management toolkit is micro-tasking.

- This approach involves breaking down a more extensive, seemingly impossible task into smaller, more manageable pieces.
- These micro-tasks are less intimidating and quick to complete, providing frequent moments of accomplishment that boost morale and motivation.
- For example, if you need to clean your office, start organizing your desk, move on to a bookshelf, and continue in these manageable increments.
- This method makes the task feel less overwhelming and creates a series of achievable goals that can help maintain focus and momentum.

Visual progress indicators can be incredibly powerful tools for enhancing the benefits of micro-tasking. Humans are naturally visual creatures. We derive satisfaction from seeing evidence of our progress.

- Tools like progress bars or simple checklists can be very motivating. For instance, you use a checklist for the office cleaning, ticking off each area as completed.
- Digital tools and apps that provide visual cues, such as filling bars or completing circles, can also give this visual feedback.
- Each small task completed and checked off sends a little dopamine rush to your brain, a reward signal that can help keep you engaged and less likely to give in to procrastination.

Moreover, turning task completion into a game through timed challenges can add an element of fun and urgency that might be missing otherwise.

- This gamification of tasks works well for the ADHD brain, stimulated by novelty and urgency.
- You can set a timer for a small burst of focused activity — say, 10 minutes. Challenge yourself to see how much of a task you can complete in that time.
- This method not only helps manage time perception — a common issue in ADHD — but also injects a playful competitive element into mundane activities, making them more engaging and less likely to be put off.

These strategies — micro-tasking, using visual progress indicators, and setting timed challenges — are not just tools to manage procrastination; they are steps toward reclaiming your agency over your tasks and your time.

- By breaking tasks down into smaller pieces, visually tracking your progress, and adding elements of timed competition, you transform overwhelming challenges into a series of victories.
- This approach doesn't just reduce procrastination; it enhances your overall productivity and sense of accomplishment, paving the way for a more structured and rewarding management of tasks.

1.7 CREATING ADHD-FRIENDLY DAILY ROUTINES

The concept of establishing a daily routine might evoke a yawn from some, but for those navigating life with ADHD, it's a game-changer. Routines can significantly reduce the mental load of decision-making, which is a real challenge when your brain is juggling countless thoughts and tasks.

- Think of a routine as a framework that supports your day, not as chains restricting your freedom.
- It provides structure but is flexible enough to adapt to the unexpected twists that are all too common with ADHD.
- This structure can improve efficiency and reduce stress, allowing more mental space for creativity and spontaneity throughout the day.

Creating a routine that works for ADHD involves understanding that our energy levels and focus fluctuate significantly, meaning that a one-size-fits-all approach is less likely to be successful.

- Instead, consider developing customizable routine templates that adapt to your mood on a given day or the tasks that need priority.
- For instance, you might have a template for high-energy days, another for average days, and a third for low-energy days.
- Each template could suggest different tasks or vary the intensity and duration according to your energy levels.

Incorporating flexibility into these routines is crucial. While it might seem counterintuitive, flexibility makes routines sustainable for someone with ADHD.

- Routines could include blocks of time reserved for high-priority tasks but also open periods during which you can choose what you feel most inclined to work on.
- This method respects the natural ebb and flow of your attention and interest, which are hallmark traits of ADHD.
- It's about finding the balance between having enough structure to guide you and enough freedom to

accommodate the natural variability in your focus and energy.

It is equally essential to maintain and adjust these routines over time. Life changes, and so will your needs and responsibilities.

- Regularly review your routines every few months or when a major life event occurs.

    ○ Ask yourself what's working and what isn't.
    ○ Are there new tasks that need to be incorporated?
    ○ Are there routines that have become stale or no longer serve your goals?

- Adjusting your routines isn't a sign of failure. It's a proactive way to ensure they continue serving you well.
- It's also helpful to keep a routine journal to jot down what you've tried, what's worked, what hasn't, and any ideas you have for adjustments.
- A journal can be a valuable resource when it's time to tweak your routines.

Establishing and maintaining a routine when you have ADHD isn't about imposing strict rules on yourself—it's about creating a supportive framework that accommodates your unique way of experiencing the world. It's about making your day smoother, not rigid. With the right approach, routines can be a powerful tool for managing ADHD.

- They can help you harness your energy and direct it to what matters most.
- They reduce the daily decision fatigue that can be exhausting and free up more space to enjoy life.

- The goal is to create a routine that feels like it's working for you, not one that you constantly struggle to keep up with.
- Remember, the best routine is one that you'll stick to, one that supports your goals and respects your limits.
- So, take the time to craft routines that make sense for you, and be ready to adapt them as you learn more about what helps you thrive.

Exhibit 1
Eisenhower Matrix

	URGENT	NOT URGENT
Important	**DO IMMEDIATELY** UPCOMING DEADLINES EMERGENCIES Quadrant I	**SCHEDULE** EXERCISING LONG TERM PROJECTS OVERALL GOALS CALLING FRIENDS Quadrant II
Not Important	**DELEGATE/AVOID** INTERRUPTIONS CERTAIN PHONE CALLS DISTRACTIONS OTHER'S PRIORITIES Quadrant III	**DO LATER/AVOID** WATCHING NETFLIX CHECKING SOCIAL MEDIA PLAYING VIDEO GAMES Quadrant IV

Urgent vs. Important

Urgent Tasks require your immediate attention. These tasks put you in a hurried mindset & generate stress.

Important tasks help you achieve long-term goals. To know what things are actually important, you first have to figure out your own goals.

Benefits

- It helps to prioritize complex or unclear issues when there are multiple criteria for determining importance.
- It provides a quick and easy, yet consistent method for evaluating options.
- It is adaptable for many priority setting needs like projects, services, personnel, etc.

Apps

- Focus Matrix
- Priority Matrix
- Custom TaskIt

Quadrants of the Eisenhower Matrix

Quadrant I: Important and Urgent

These are the activities that you have to do right away: crises, problems, or deadlines. These are tasks that were in Quadrant II and we kept pushing away until they became urgent. Even though tasks will always come up that are important and urgent, to reduce them, we can take more time doing the tasks from Quadrant II.

Quadrant II: Important and Not Urgent

These are tasks that help us achieve long term goals but do not have a pressing deadline (ex. studying for an exam in two weeks). These tasks can move to Quadrant I if not completed. Personal and self-care tasks fall into Quadrant II.
It is important to first take care of Quadrant I and then Quadrant II. These Quadrant II tasks can be broken down over a period of time. Avoid stress & poor work quality by completing these tasks before they move to Quadrant I.

Quadrant III: Not Important and Urgent

These tasks require our attention right now, but do not help us achieve our goals. These tasks look like interruptions from other people or favors; they're often time-consuming. They are not necessarily bad, but they need to be balanced with activities from Quadrants I and II. The solution is to become more assertive and start to politely say no so you can focus on your priorities.

Quadrant IV: Not Important and Not Urgent

These tasks are mostly distractions and could take up most of the day if not moderated. These activities do not have to be eliminated, but should be pushed until other important tasks are completed. After a busy day, watching TV or going on social media can help you relax. Just make sure that they are not taking most of your day!

Created by Maria Spinetti
Revised by Jack Crone
ACE Academic Coach
Student Learning and Academic Success

ENHANCING PERSONAL RELATIONSHIPS

Navigating the intricacies of personal relationships can often feel like trying to solve a complex puzzle, especially when ADHD is in the mix. Each interaction can sometimes seem overwhelming, with its unspoken rules and emotional nuances. Yet, relationships are also where we find joy, support, and connection. This chapter will delve into key skills that can transform how you interact with others, enhancing your relationships' depth and quality. Specifically, we'll focus on refining your active listening skills — an essential component of effective communication and a cornerstone of healthy relationships.

2.1 ACTIVE LISTENING SKILLS FOR BETTER RELATIONSHIP DYNAMICS

Practicing Mindful Listening

Mindfulness might be a buzzword you've heard tossed around quite a bit, but when it comes to listening, it's a game-changer, especially for those with ADHD.

- Mindful listening requires you to fully concentrate on what the other person is saying without letting your mind wander to what you'll say next or a different topic altogether. Mindful listening can be particularly challenging when your thoughts feel like they are moving a mile a minute.
- However, the effort to bring yourself back to the conversation each time you drift shows respect and enhances your understanding of the discussion.
- Begin by acknowledging that your mind will wander and gently guide it back to the conversation without self-judgment.
- This practice improves your listening skills and helps reduce the anxiety of conversational misunderstandings.

Clarifying and Paraphrasing

Clarification and paraphrasing are your allies in ensuring that your understanding matches what was said.

- In conversations, especially emotionally charged ones, it's easy to misinterpret words based on our mood or past experiences.

- By repeating back what you heard in your own words — "So, what I'm hearing is..." or "Do you mean that...?" — you allow the speaker to confirm or correct your understanding.
- This technique not only prevents misunderstandings common in ADHD relationships, where attention to detail might slip, but also shows the speaker that you are genuinely engaged and interested in what they say.

Nonverbal Cues and Body Language

Much of communication is nonverbal, which can sometimes be a tricky field to navigate for someone with ADHD, who might miss subtle cues.

- Paying attention to body language — facial expressions, gestures, posture — can provide significant insights into how the other person feels beyond what they say.
- Conversely, knowing your body language can help you communicate more effectively.
- Simple actions like nodding, maintaining eye contact, or leaning slightly forward can show the speaker you are actively listening.
- Practice these skills in a less pressured environment or in front of a mirror to become more aware of your natural tendencies and how they might be perceived.

Feedback Loops

Establishing a giving and requesting feedback routine can enhance communication efficacy over time.

- After important conversations, ask for feedback — "Did you feel heard?" "How could I understand you better next time?"
- This routine helps adjust your listening habits and deepens trust, showing your commitment to improving the relationship.
- Offering your feedback about how you felt during the conversation can also encourage mutual growth and understanding.
- Make this practice a regular part of your interactions, and your communication skills will likely improve significantly.

Practicing Empathy

Empathy involves more than understanding another person's feelings. It requires you to share them.

- For someone with ADHD, who might deal with emotional dysregulation, practicing empathy can be both a challenge and a profound avenue for connection.
- Start by focusing on trying to feel what the other person is feeling.
- Imagine yourself in their situation, not just on a superficial level, but sincerely, considering their emotional background and current circumstances.
- Expressing this empathy through words of affirmation or supportive actions can significantly strengthen your relationships, providing an invaluable sense of companionship and support.

Developing these active listening skills will enhance your ability to communicate effectively and deepen your connections with others, creating more fulfilling and supportive relationships.

- Whether with friends, family, or colleagues, listening actively and empathetically is foundational to building strong, lasting bonds.
- As you practice these skills, you'll likely discover improvements in your relationships with others and a greater understanding and appreciation of the diverse ways people express themselves and their needs.

2.2 COMMUNICATION STRATEGIES FOR ADHD-AFFECTED RELATIONSHIPS

In personal or professional relationships, clear and structured communication is like the compass that guides ships through foggy waters—it directs and ensures that both parties reach their intended understanding without getting lost in misunderstandings.

- When ADHD is involved, this clarity becomes even more crucial, as the typical distracted tendencies can often muddy the conversational waters.
- To navigate these challenges, adopting a method of clear, concise, and structured communication can significantly alleviate the common frustrations encountered in ADHD-affected relationships.

When communicating, especially about something important, think of your words as building blocks.

- Place each block thoughtfully and make it strong enough to stand independently.
- Be direct and to the point. Avoid tangents that ADHD so often invites.
- Structuring your conversation with clear beginnings, middles, and ends helps prevent the dialogue from spiraling.
- For instance, when discussing plans, start with the when and where discuss the why, and conclude by confirming everyone's understanding and agreement.
- This framework keeps you on track and makes it easier for the listener to follow and absorb the information.

Expressing your needs and setting boundaries is also pivotal.

- For many with ADHD, overwhelmed feelings can arise when boundaries blur.
- Communicating your needs might include explaining how your ADHD affects you in specific settings and discussing strategies that might help mitigate those impacts, such as needing brief breaks during long sessions or preferring written forms of communication for complex information.
- Techniques such as using visual aids, like diagrams or charts, can help clarify your points.
- Written agreements are also valuable; they provide a reference that can help prevent future misunderstandings and ensure that all parties remember and respect the discussed boundaries.

Regular check-ins are another key strategy.

- They serve as both preventative maintenance and tune-ups for your relationships.
- By scheduling regular times to discuss ongoing projects, feelings, or plans, you create a consistent space for communication that can help avoid the buildup of unsaid words or unresolved issues.
- These check-ins keep the dialogue flowing and make it easier to address small issues before they become bigger problems.
- Whether it's a weekly summary email to a colleague or a nightly chat with your partner about the day, these regular connections can fortify relationships against the typical communication pitfalls that ADHD might throw your way.

Lastly, integrating communication tools and aids can streamline interactions and reduce the cognitive load often accompanying ADHD.

- Reminder apps, for instance, can be lifesavers for keeping track of important dates, meetings, or discussions.
- They relieve memory pressure, allowing you to focus more on the content of interactions rather than worrying about remembering them.
- Shared digital calendars are another excellent tool for coordinating schedules with partners or team members.
- They allow everyone involved to see, add, and adjust plans as needed, ensuring everyone is informed and last-minute changes do not blindside anyone.

By adopting these strategies — clear communication, expressing needs and boundaries, regular check-ins, and utilizing helpful tools — you can significantly improve how you connect with others, making your relationships more fulfilling and less stressful. These methods not only accommodate the challenges posed by ADHD but also enrich your interactions, allowing you to build stronger, more understanding connections with those around you.

2.3 MANAGING EMOTIONAL DYSREGULATION WITH LOVED ONES

Emotions can feel like a rollercoaster ride, especially when ADHD is in the driver's seat.

- Emotional dysregulation, a common challenge for those with ADHD, can make feelings seem more intense, unpredictable, and difficult to manage.
- This challenge can strain your most important relationships with family, friends, and partners.
- Understanding and managing these emotional nuances can significantly improve interpersonal dynamics, creating a more stable and supportive environment for everyone involved.

Identifying Triggers

The first step toward managing emotional dysregulation is identifying what triggers these intense emotional responses.

- Triggers can vary widely. They might be specific situations, words, actions, or even people.
- For someone with ADHD, common triggers could include feeling overwhelmed by too many demands, facing criticism, or experiencing failure.

- Start by keeping a mood journal, noting instances where you felt a sudden emotional shift.
- Record the situation, the people involved, and the discussion topic.
- Over time, patterns will likely emerge, highlighting specific triggers.
- Recognizing these triggers is crucial as it allows you to anticipate and prepare for potentially challenging situations, reducing the likelihood of an emotional spike.

Communication During Emotional Peaks

When emotions peak, communication can become a battlefield if not handled with care.

- Establishing strategies for maintaining clarity and calm before these peaks occur is essential.
- One effective method is to agree on 'time-out' signals with loved ones beforehand.
- This signal could be a simple gesture or a word that communicates the need to pause the conversation, allowing all parties to step back and regain composure.
- Everyone involved should respect this signal. When someone invokes the time-out, the conversation should pause immediately, no questions asked.
- This break can provide a crucial cooling-off period, preventing the situation from escalating further and allowing each person to reflect on the discussion more objectively.

Emotional Self-Regulation Techniques

Developing a toolkit of emotional self-regulation techniques can provide immediate relief in moments of high stress or emotional overwhelm.

- Techniques such as deep breathing, where you focus on taking slow, deliberate breaths, can help calm the nervous system and reduce the intensity of your emotional state.
- Meditation, even practiced for a few minutes a day, can increase your overall emotional resilience, making intense feelings more manageable when they do arise.
- Numerous apps are also available to aid in emotional regulation; these might offer guided breathing exercises, mindfulness practices, or short meditations tailored to relieve stress. Integrating these practices into your daily routine can enhance your ability to manage emotional peaks more effectively when they occur.

Role of Professional Help

Despite best efforts, emotional dysregulation sometimes poses significant challenges, impacting relationships and overall quality of life.

- In such cases, seeking professional help can be vital to improvement.
- Therapies like Cognitive Behavioral Therapy (CBT) are particularly effective for those with ADHD.
- CBT focuses on changing unhelpful cognitive distortions and behaviors, improving emotional regulation, and developing personal coping strategies that target solving current problems.

- A therapist specialized in ADHD can offer insights and strategies tailored specifically to navigate the complexities of ADHD-related emotional challenges.
- Remember, seeking help is a sign of strength and a proactive step toward building healthier, more fulfilling relationships.

Navigating emotional dysregulation requires patience, understanding, and proactive management.

- By identifying your triggers, establishing clear communication strategies during emotional peaks, regularly practicing emotional self-regulation techniques, and seeking professional guidance, you can create a more stable and supportive environment for yourself and your loved ones.
- These steps are not just about managing moments of intense emotion; they're about enhancing the overall quality of your relationships, ensuring they are resilient, supportive, and deeply rewarding.

2.4 BUILDING AND MAINTAINING FRIENDSHIPS WITH ADHD

Friendships are one of life's greatest joys and sources of support, particularly when navigating the ups and downs of ADHD.

- However, maintaining these relationships requires a bit more finesse and understanding, especially when it comes to communicating the nuances of your ADHD in a way that builds empathy rather than defensiveness.
- Explaining ADHD to your friends is crucial. It helps

demystify your actions and reactions and avoid misunderstandings.

- Start these conversations openly, focusing on how ADHD impacts your life rather than a clinical definition.
- Share specific instances where ADHD affects your daily interactions, like forgetting appointments or struggling to stay focused in conversations.
- This approach not only personalizes the information but also makes it more relatable.
- Ensure your tone conveys that this sharing enhances understanding and not as an excuse for shortcomings.
- Such heartfelt conversations can set a strong foundation for empathy and support, making your friends allies in your journey.

For many with ADHD, picking up on social cues or maintaining appropriate social behaviors can be challenging.

- Social skills training can be a transformative step toward building stronger friendships.
- These training sessions, often led by therapists or specialized coaches, focus on enhancing your ability to effectively interpret and respond to social cues.
- They can provide practical strategies for initiating and maintaining conversations, reading body language, and managing social anxiety.
- The skills learned can boost your confidence in social settings, making interactions more enjoyable and less stressful.
- Consider group sessions, which offer the added benefit of practicing new skills in real time with others who understand the struggle.

- This safe environment can be incredibly supportive and informative.

Planning social activities that align with your ADHD can also significantly improve your social experiences.

- Choose inherently dynamic and engaging activities like interactive games, sports, or hands-on projects like art workshops or cooking classes.
- These activities naturally keep your attention engaged and reduce the likelihood of distraction.
- Plus, they can be a lot of fun, making socializing something to look forward to rather than stress over.
- When organizing these activities, use digital calendars or event planning apps to keep track of the details.
- Setting reminders for yourself and others can help manage forgetfulness or last-minute confusion about the plans.
- By taking charge of organizing, you ensure the activities are ADHD-friendly and show your friends your commitment to maintaining your relationship.

Maintaining friendships requires consistent effort, especially when ADHD is in play.

- Regular communication is key. Simple check-ins via text or calls can keep the connection alive even when busy schedules get in the way.
- Share your interests and encourage your friends to do the same; this mutual exchange keeps the relationship balanced and engaging.
- It's also important to be upfront about the ways ADHD might affect your friendship, such as potential forgetfulness or difficulty with time management.

- Discussing ADHD traits can prevent misunderstandings and build trust.
- Setting up systems to manage these ADHD impacts can be helpful, like shared reminders for upcoming events or important dates.
- Remember, true friends will appreciate your honesty and effort. These strategies can help maintain and strengthen your friendships.

By embracing these strategies, you're not just navigating the challenges of ADHD but actively enriching your friendships.

- Through understanding, training, thoughtful planning, and consistent effort, you create a supportive network that celebrates your strengths and supports you through any challenges.
- These relationships can provide incredible emotional support through mutual respect and understanding, making your ADHD journey a shared adventure rather than a solitary struggle.

2.5 NAVIGATING SOCIAL OBLIGATIONS WITH EASE

Attending social events can be both exciting and daunting, especially when you have ADHD.

- The stimulation and interaction, while enjoyable, can also become overwhelming without the right strategies in place.
- Preparing for these events involves more than choosing the right outfit or gift. It also means preparing your mind and strategies for handling the social dynamics you'll encounter.

- One effective method is pre-planning conversation topics.
- Before attending an event, take some time to think about potential topics of interest to discuss.
- This preparation can ease the pressure of thinking on your feet, which can be more challenging in noisy or crowded environments.
- Additionally, relaxation techniques before heading out — such as deep breathing exercises or a short meditation session — can significantly lower your stress levels and improve your ability to interact calmly and enjoyably.

When you're at a social function, it's common to experience over-stimulation due to the bustling environment — music, multiple conversations, clinking glasses. All these can quickly become sensory overload.

- Recognizing the early signs of sensory overload is crucial in managing your response.
- These signs might include feeling unusually irritable, having trouble following conversations, or needing to escape.
- Once you recognize these signs, you can implement strategies to manage the situation.
- Carrying noise-canceling headphones or stepping outside for a few minutes to get fresh air can be immensely helpful.
- Having a plan in place for such situations is also beneficial, which might include a quiet spot away from the crowd where you can decompress.

Social scripts and role-playing can be particularly beneficial for improving interaction and easing anxiety in social settings.

- Before an event, practice greeting people, joining a group conversation, or politely removing yourself.
- You can role-play these scenarios with a friend or in front of a mirror.
- This practice can boost your confidence and reduce anxiety about social interactions.
- It equips you with a mental toolbox of phrases and actions that feel natural and appropriate, making the social experience less daunting and more enjoyable.

Finally, having a set of polite and effective exit strategies can be essential, especially when events become overwhelming or conflict with your other responsibilities.

- It's helpful to pre-plan your exit by setting a time limit for your stay or arranging responsibilities that require leaving at a certain time.
- Communicating your plans early in the conversations can also prevent any awkwardness when the moment to leave arrives.
- A simple "I'm enjoying this, but I'll have to leave by nine to catch up on some work" sets the stage early, allowing you to exit smoothly without misunderstandings.

By integrating these strategies — pre-planning conversations, managing overstimulation, practicing social scripts, and having clear exit strategies — you can navigate social obligations with greater ease and confidence. These preparations make socializing less stressful and enjoyable, allowing you to engage fully without feeling overwhelmed or out of place.

2.6 BUILDING TRUST AND UNDERSTANDING IN PARTNERSHIPS

Trust is the foundation that builds any partnership, be it in love, friendship, or collaboration.

- For those navigating the waters of ADHD, this foundational trust includes a deep understanding of how ADHD can uniquely color our perceptions and actions.
- Transparency about your ADHD challenges is not just about sharing what your struggles are but also about opening up on how these might influence your relationship dynamics.
- It's about letting someone in on why you might forget dates seem disorganized, or need more time to process information, which isn't always easy.
- This kind of openness can foster a supportive environment where misunderstandings are less likely to take root and empathy flourishes.

Cultivating this transparency means more than an occasional heart-to-heart during conflict or confusion.

- It involves a consistent effort to communicate openly about your daily experiences with ADHD.
- These communication topics involve discussing how specific environments or conversations affect your mood and focus or explaining how you might react to unexpected changes or stress.
- It's important, though, to balance these discussions with reassurance that you are actively managing your ADHD, which can prevent your partner from feeling overwhelmed or responsible for your challenges.

- This ongoing dialogue helps to demystify your experiences and invites your partner to be a supportive ally.

Establishing shared goals and values can further solidify the bonds of your partnership.

- When both partners understand and agree on what they are collectively striving toward, it becomes easier to navigate the ups and downs that ADHD might bring into the relationship.
- Start by identifying areas in your relationship where your goals intersect, be it financial security, family planning, or personal growth.
- Setting these common objectives aligns your efforts and gives you a clear roadmap, reducing potential conflicts arising from misaligned expectations.
- Regular discussions about these goals ensure that both partners remain on the same page and can make adjustments as circumstances change.

Regular relationship assessments can be incredibly beneficial in maintaining the health of your partnership.

- Think of these like tune-ups for your relationship.
- Set aside time every few months to check in on various aspects of your relationship.
- Discuss what's working well and what might need adjustment.
- Approach these assessments without judgment, focusing on understanding and growth rather than criticism.
- These conversations can cover everything from daily communication habits to emotional intimacy and help

address minor grievances before they become more significant.

- They also reinforce the idea that the relationship is a priority for both of you, deserving of time and attention to flourish.

Lastly, educating yourselves can be a powerful tool in navigating ADHD in your partnership.

- There are numerous resources available that can help deepen both partners' understanding of ADHD.
- These can range from books and articles to seminars and workshops.
- For a partner without ADHD, these resources can provide valuable insights into how ADHD affects relationships and offer practical advice on supporting a partner with ADHD.
- For someone with ADHD, these resources can offer self-management strategies and tips on communicating your needs effectively.
- Learning about ADHD together equips you both with the knowledge to handle the challenges and shows a mutual commitment to understanding and supporting each other.

By embracing transparency, setting shared goals, regularly assessing your relationship, and educating yourselves about ADHD, you create a resilient partnership in the face of challenges and deeply enrich mutual understanding and respect. In such a partnership, ADHD becomes a part of the journey you navigate together, with empathy and support guiding your way. This approach does not just benefit the relationship but also contributes to personal growth and mutual fulfillment.

2.7 ADDRESSING REJECTION SENSITIVE DYSPHORIA (RSD)

Rejection Sensitive Dysphoria (RSD) is a term that might not be familiar to everyone. Still, for many adults with ADHD, it encapsulates a profound and often painful aspect of their emotional experience.

- RSD is intense emotional sensitivity and pain triggered by the perception of rejection or criticism.
- Even a slight hint of disapproval or the mere assumption of rejection can send someone with RSD into a spiral of overwhelming emotions.
- For those with ADHD, who may already be dealing with emotional dysregulation, RSD can feel like an unmanageable amplification of every negative interaction, however minor it might be.

Managing RSD effectively starts with understanding its triggers and nature.

- It's not uncommon for individuals with RSD to misinterpret or exaggerate situations as being critically negative when they might not be.
- One helpful strategy is reality-checking your thoughts.
- This strategy involves taking a step back from your emotional response and assessing the situation objectively.
- Ask yourself, "What evidence do I have that this person is rejecting me?" or "Could there be another explanation for this reaction?"
- This method helps to put distance between your immediate emotional response and the reality of the

situation, providing a chance to reassess and respond more proportionately.

Emotional desensitization techniques can also be beneficial.

- These techniques involve gradually exposing yourself to the fear of rejection in controlled, manageable doses.
- This technique could be as simple as asking questions you fear might be silly or requesting small favors from friends or family that you worry might be denied.
- Over time, these small exposures can reduce the intensity of the emotional response associated with rejection, making it easier to cope with more extensive, more significant situations.
- Additionally, setting realistic expectations for social interactions is crucial.
- Understand that not every interaction will go perfectly and that feeling uncomfortable or anxious about rejection is okay.
- Accepting these as part of the human experience rather than as personal failures can significantly reduce the stress associated with RSD.

Discussing RSD with those close to you can also make a significant difference.

- Opening up about such vulnerabilities can be difficult, but sharing your experience with friends, family, and coworkers can lead to greater understanding and support.
- Explain what RSD is and how it affects you, describing it as an allergic reaction to perceived rejection or criticism.
- Let them know how they can help, which could be as

simple as providing clear and direct feedback or offering reassurance in situations where you might feel judged.

- Open communication can help build a supportive network that recognizes and accommodates your sensitivity, potentially reducing the frequency and intensity of RSD episodes.

Professional help can be a valuable resource for those who find it particularly challenging to manage RSD through self-help strategies alone.

- Therapeutic approaches, particularly Cognitive Behavioral Therapy (CBT), have been effective in helping individuals understand and alter the thought patterns that contribute to RSD.
- CBT can teach you to recognize distorted thoughts about rejection and replace them with more realistic and constructive thoughts, thereby reducing the emotional impact.
- In some cases, medication may also be recommended by a professional to help manage the intense emotions and anxiety that come with RSD.
- It's important to consult with a healthcare provider who understands ADHD and RSD to discuss the most effective and suitable treatment options.

Navigating RSD requires patience, understanding, and often a multi-faceted approach involving personal strategies, open communication, and possibly professional intervention.

- Addressing RSD with thoughtful and informed tactics can diminish its impact on your life, leading to more stable and

satisfying interpersonal relationships and a better quality of life.
- Understanding and managing this complex emotional response is not just about reducing pain, it's about moving toward a more balanced and fulfilling emotional landscape.

2.8 CONFLICT RESOLUTION SKILLS FOR ADULTS WITH ADHD

Conflict is a natural part of any relationship, but for adults with ADHD, the usual turbulence can feel like navigating a storm.

- Recognizing patterns in conflicts that often arise in relationships affected by ADHD can dramatically change how you handle disagreements and misunderstandings.
- Typically, these patterns might include impulsively reacting rather than responding thoughtfully or struggling to pay attention during heated discussions, which can further escalate conflicts.
- Seeing these patterns for what they are — a part of your ADHD and not a character flaw — allows you to approach conflicts with more awareness and strategies tailored to mitigate these tendencies.

One of the most effective ways to keep communication clear and calm during conflicts is using "I" statements.

- This technique shifts the focus from blaming the other person to expressing your feelings and needs.
- For example, instead of saying, "You never listen to me," you might say, "I feel frustrated when I think I'm not being heard."

- This small shift can significantly reduce the conversation's defensiveness, making it easier for both parties to engage constructively.
- Additionally, timed breaks during conflicts can be incredibly beneficial, especially when emotions run high.
- Setting a timer for a five-minute break gives everyone involved a chance to breathe, collect their thoughts, and cool down, making it more likely to find a resolution upon returning.

Problem-solving during conflicts doesn't have to be a battleground.

- Structured problem-solving strategies can turn these moments into opportunities for growth and understanding.
- Begin by clearly defining the problem without blame, then brainstorm possible solutions.
- Evaluate these solutions objectively, discuss the pros and cons of each, and mutually decide on the best course of action.
- This structured approach keeps the conversation focused and encourages collaborative problem-solving, which can strengthen the relationship in the long run.

Post-conflict, repairing the relationship is crucial for maintaining long-term harmony.

- Sincere apologies, where necessary, can go a long way in mending hurt feelings.
- These apologies must acknowledge specific actions and their impacts rather than vague or dismissive statements.

- Reaffirming your commitment to the relationship and better handling such situations in the future also reinforces trust and security between you and your loved ones.
- Lastly, discussing concrete steps to prevent future conflicts shows a proactive commitment to improving the relationship.
- Whether committing to using "I" statements more regularly or agreeing to take timed breaks during heated discussions, these actionable plans can help ensure that the same issues don't repeat.

Navigating conflicts with skill and care alleviates the immediate stress associated with arguments and builds trust and understanding that enriches your relationships. By recognizing common conflict patterns related to ADHD — utilizing calm communication techniques, embracing structured problem-solving, and taking steps to repair relationships post-conflict — you empower yourself and your loved ones to handle disagreements in ways that strengthen rather than strain your bonds.

As this chapter wraps up, we've explored the dynamics of enhancing personal relationships through understanding ADHD-related challenges, effective communication, emotional regulation, and conflict resolution. These insights are not just about making life smoother; they're about deepening connections and fostering environments where you and your relationships can thrive. As we transition into the next chapter, we'll focus on optimizing workplace interactions and environments, leveraging your understanding of ADHD to survive and thrive in professional settings.

NAVIGATING PROFESSIONAL RELATIONSHIPS

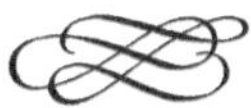

Stepping into your workspace isn't just a collection of desks and computers. It's a dynamic arena where professional relationships are built and maintained. For those with Adult ADHD, this environment presents both unique challenges and opportunities. Navigating these waters can significantly influence your career trajectory and workplace satisfaction. This chapter delves into one of the pivotal aspects of professional interactions for individuals with ADHD, the disclosure of your condition in the workplace. Deciding if, when, and how to disclose your ADHD can feel like navigating a labyrinth. Still, with the right approach, this process can become a strategic step toward crafting a supportive work environment.

3.1 DISCLOSURE OF ADHD IN THE WORKPLACE: WHEN AND HOW

Evaluating the Benefits and Risks

Deciding whether to disclose your ADHD at work is a decision layered with potential benefits and risks.

- On the one hand, sharing your diagnosis can pave the way for access to accommodations that can significantly improve your work performance and reduce daily stress.
- It can foster understanding from supervisors and colleagues, which can be invaluable in building supportive professional relationships.
- On the other hand, the stigma surrounding ADHD means that disclosure could potentially lead to biases or, worse, affect your career advancement opportunities due to misconceptions about your capabilities.

Weighing these pros and cons requires a nuanced understanding of your workplace culture and needs.

- If your work environment champions inclusivity and mental health awareness, the risk of facing stigma may be lower, and the benefits outweigh the risks.
- However, disclosing might require careful consideration in more traditional or less inclusive environments.
- It's also crucial to assess how much your ADHD impacts your work.
- If ADHD significantly affects your performance, the accommodations that come with disclosure could be crucial for your professional success.

Choosing the Right Moment

Timing is everything when it comes to disclosure. You should strategically choose the ideal time to share your diagnosis to foster understanding and support.

- One practical approach is to disclose your ADHD during a performance review period, especially if you've been performing well.
- This context allows you to present your ADHD, not as an excuse for any shortcomings but as an explanation that might help optimize your future performance.
- Alternatively, waiting to establish a good work record can also be strategic.
- Once you've demonstrated your value and capabilities, your colleagues and supervisors may be more likely to respond to your disclosure with support rather than skepticism.

How to Disclose Effectively

Disclosing your ADHD at the right time is about more than just sharing your diagnosis; it's about advocating for yourself and educating others about what ADHD means in a professional context.

- Start by preparing what you want to say ahead of time.
- It can be helpful to script out your key points, focusing on how ADHD affects your work and what specific accommodations could assist you in fulfilling your job role more effectively.
- For example, you might say, "I have ADHD, which sometimes makes it hard for me to manage my time

effectively. A flexible schedule or a quiet workspace could help me perform at my best."
- Be clear and concise, and avoid overly medicalized language that might confuse your listener. Instead, focus on practical implications and solutions.

Legal Rights and Protections

Understanding your legal rights is crucial when disclosing ADHD in the workplace.

- In the United States, the Americans with Disabilities Act (ADA) protects against discrimination for individuals with disabilities, including those with ADHD.
- ADA guidelines entitle you to reasonable accommodations that help you perform your job, provided they do not impose an undue hardship on the business.
- Before disclosing, familiarize yourself with these protections and consider discussing your rights with a human resources representative or legal advisor.
- This knowledge empowers you and equips you with the tools to negotiate the accommodations you need to thrive professionally.

Navigating the disclosure of ADHD in the workplace is a complex but navigable challenge.

- By carefully weighing the benefits and risks, choosing the right moment, communicating effectively, and understanding your legal rights, you can make an informed decision that supports your professional growth and well-being.

- This proactive approach enhances your work environment and contributes to a broader understanding and acceptance of ADHD in the professional world.

3.2 STRATEGIES FOR EFFECTIVE TEAM COLLABORATION

When you're part of a team, understanding everyone's role and the expectations of each member can sometimes feel like solving a complex puzzle, especially when ADHD is part of your daily reality.

- Clarity in roles and expectations is not just beneficial, it's essential.
- It helps prevent the all-too-common scenarios where tasks overlap or, conversely, fall through the cracks entirely.
- For someone with ADHD, this clarity is even more critical, as it provides a structured framework that can help manage the often overwhelming flood of duties and responsibilities.
- It's essential to initiate or request clear discussions about role delineation and expectations at the onset of projects and during regular team meetings.
- These discussions could outline specific responsibilities associated with each role and discuss the expectations that team members have of one another.
- Such clarity not only aids in holding each member accountable but also supports you in managing your tasks more effectively by allowing you to understand precisely where your responsibilities begin and end, reducing the anxiety that often comes with ambiguity.

Project management tools and apps can significantly streamline team collaboration, making it easier to track tasks, deadlines, and responsibilities.

- These tools are particularly beneficial for managing the common organizational challenges associated with ADHD, such as keeping track of multiple tasks and deadlines across various projects.
- Platforms like **Asana**, **Trello**, or **Monday.com** allow you to visualize tasks in a user-friendly interface, where you can see the specific task or subtask, who is responsible for what, and when tasks are due.
- These tools often offer features like setting reminders, updating task status, and tagging team members, which can help keep you engaged and proactive in your contributions.
- Integrating these tools into your daily workflow can help mitigate feelings of overwhelm and enhance your ability to contribute effectively to team projects.

Regular check-ins or stand-up meetings are also crucial for maintaining open and consistent communication within the team.

- These meetings provide a regular platform for discussing project progress, addressing concerns, and recalibrating goals.
- For someone with ADHD, these regular touchpoints can be particularly valuable.
- They offer an opportunity to clarify any confusion about tasks, provide updates on your progress, and receive immediate feedback.
- This consistent engagement helps maintain focus on the

project objectives and can significantly enhance one's sense of involvement and accomplishment.

- Furthermore, these meetings can foster a culture of transparency and mutual support, where team members feel more connected and committed to the project's success.

Creating a supportive team environment is perhaps one of the most crucial elements for effective collaboration, especially for workers with ADHD.

- Encourage an atmosphere where team members can ask for help or clarification without judgment.
- Promoting empathy and understanding within the team can foster a positive environment. Team-building activities or discussions about workplace diversity and inclusion can create the proper environment.
- Such an environment benefits individuals with ADHD by providing the support they need to manage their unique challenges, and it also enhances the team's overall cohesiveness and adaptive capacity.
- When team members feel supported, they are more likely to perform well, engage meaningfully with their tasks, and contribute positively to the team dynamics.

These strategies for effective team collaboration are not just about making your work life easier. They're about enhancing the quality and output of your team.

- Clarifying roles and expectations, utilizing practical tools, maintaining regular communication, and fostering a supportive environment can transform your team's operations.

- These changes can lead to more efficient project completion, a more harmonious work environment, and a more satisfying professional experience for everyone involved, especially those managing ADHD in the workplace.

3.3 DEALING WITH CRITICISM AND FEEDBACK AT WORK

Receiving feedback, especially when it points out areas of improvement, can sometimes feel like a personal critique rather than a professional one.

- If you're dealing with ADHD, with heightened emotional sensitivity, any criticism can feel personal.
- However, it's crucial to learn techniques to depersonalize criticism, viewing it as an opportunity for growth rather than a reflection of one's self-worth.
- When feedback comes your way, try to see it through the lens of your role, not your identity.
- Remind yourself that the feedback is about your work output or behavior in a professional capacity, not about you as a person.
- Mental separation can reduce the sting of criticism and allow you to focus on the objective points.

One effective way to handle feedback is to approach it with a learning mindset.

- When receiving feedback, give yourself time to process the information.
- Take a few moments during the feedback session to

breathe and gather your thoughts, or even ask to revisit the feedback after you've had time to reflect on it.
- This process time is crucial for managing ADHD-related impulsivity, where an immediate reaction may be defensive.
- Once you've had time to reflect, revisit the feedback, focusing on understanding the key points.
- If certain aspects are unclear, ask clarifying questions to ensure you fully understand the feedback before responding or considering changes.

Formulating an improvement plan based on feedback is another constructive step.

- This plan should include specific, achievable goals.
- For instance, if the feedback was about your meeting punctuality, a goal might be to set reminders for yourself 10 minutes before every meeting to start wrapping up whatever you're working on.
- By setting clear and achievable goals, you can methodically address the areas of improvement identified in the feedback. This method can help mitigate the overwhelm and helplessness associated with tackling too much at once.

Proactively soliciting feedback can also be a game-changer, especially for managing ADHD at work.

- Instead of waiting for feedback to come to you — often at scheduled reviews or after something has gone wrong — regularly ask for feedback on specific tasks or projects.
- This approach shows your commitment to continuous

improvement and helps you gather more directed and manageable feedback.

- It can reduce anxiety associated with receiving feedback, as it becomes a regular part of your routine rather than a dreaded, sporadic event.
- Additionally, by soliciting feedback proactively, you can guide the feedback process, focusing on areas you are currently working to improve or that you feel particularly uncertain about.

When approached with the right strategies, feedback can be a powerful tool for professional growth.

- By separating yourself from the situation, processing the feedback thoughtfully, asking clarifying questions, and proactively seeking feedback, you transform potentially challenging interactions into opportunities for personal and professional development.
- These steps allow you to take control of your growth process, making feedback sessions less about evaluation and more about constructive evolution in your professional role.
- This proactive and structured approach to handling feedback can significantly enhance your effectiveness at work, turning what might once have been a source of stress into a cornerstone of your professional development.

3.4 ENHANCING WORKPLACE COMMUNICATION WITH ADHD

In the bustling hive of any workplace, effective communication is the glue that holds everything together.

- For those with ADHD and issues with memory, attention, and organizational skills, the usual challenges of workplace communication can be more difficult.
- Adopting structured communication methods can significantly alleviate these challenges.
- Regular briefings, for instance, are a fantastic way to keep everyone on the same page.
- By scheduling brief daily or weekly meetings, you can ensure that all team members, including yourself, are updated on project statuses, upcoming deadlines, and any shifts in priorities.
- These briefings provide a regular touchpoint that can help manage the forgetfulness and distractibility that often accompany ADHD.
- Moreover, supplementing verbal briefings with written summaries can help reinforce the information shared, providing a readily accessible reference.
- This dual approach caters to learning and retention styles and can be especially helpful if information tends to "slip through the cracks" in your memory.

Adapting your communication style to fit your listeners' preferences can also dramatically improve how your messages are received and understood.

- This adaptation is crucial in a professional setting where clarity and effectiveness are paramount.

- For instance, if you are presenting to a senior executive known for making fast-paced decisions, you might focus on delivering concise, bullet-pointed information that gets straight to the point.
- Conversely, providing comprehensive background information and data might be more appropriate when collaborating with a detail-oriented colleague.
- Tuning into these stylistic preferences can help you communicate more effectively, ensuring your ideas and input are heard and truly understood.
- These changes help build professional relationships and enhance your effectiveness and confidence in your role.

Visual aids can be pivotal in enhancing your communication efforts, especially given the propensity for visual learning many with ADHD experience.

- Incorporating charts, graphs, or slides in presentations or meetings can help maintain your audience's attention and make the information more digestible.
- Visual aids act as anchor points that can help guide your presentation and discussion, ensuring you communicate key points clearly and effectively.
- They also serve as excellent tools for keeping your focus centered during presentations, providing a structured pathway through your material to manage the distractibility that might otherwise lead you off course.

Mindfulness practices have gained traction in many personal and professional development areas, and their application in enhancing communication skills is particularly beneficial for individuals with ADHD.

- Mindfulness in listening and speaking involves being fully present in the moment, a practice that can help manage the impulsivity and rapid thought processes characteristic of ADHD.
- Before entering a meeting or conversation, taking a moment to center yourself with a few deep breaths can help clear your mind and increase your focus.
- During conversations, listen actively without planning your response while the other person is still talking.
- This focus can improve your understanding of the discussion and lead to more thoughtful and effective responses.
- Regular mindfulness practice can transform your approach to communication, making your interactions more engaging and productive.
- These skills are not merely about managing ADHD symptoms; they are about enhancing your overall ability to communicate personally and professionally, leading to improved relationships and greater success in your career endeavors.

3.5 BUILDING AND LEVERAGING WORKPLACE RELATIONSHIPS

Creating robust workplace relationships is crucial for career advancement and making daily professional life enjoyable and productive, especially when managing ADHD.

- Effective networking within your workplace can open doors to valuable mentorship, forge alliances, and garner the support necessary to thrive.
- Start by identifying individuals in your organization

whose career paths or skills you admire and seek ways to connect with them.

- Create connections by joining committee projects, attending company social events, or even scheduling informal coffee meetings to learn about others' experiences and share your aspirations.
- For those with ADHD, who might sometimes feel out of step in social settings, preparing some topics of conversation beforehand can ease the anxiety around these interactions.
- Focus on listening actively during these interactions, showing genuine interest in the other person's experiences and feedback. This effort will help form a connection that goes beyond mere acquaintance.

Collaboration in the workplace is another area where individuals with ADHD can truly shine, thanks to their often innate creativity and problem-solving skills.

- When embarking on team projects, openly advocate for roles that allow you to tap into these strengths.
- Propose innovative solutions during brainstorming sessions or take on tasks that require out-of-the-box thinking.
- However, it's also important to acknowledge and manage the aspects of ADHD that might pose challenges, such as time management or sustained focus.
- By leveraging project management tools or breaking tasks into smaller, manageable parts, you can ensure these challenges are consistent with your unique skills.
- This proactive approach enhances your contribution to the team and positions you as a competent and innovative team player.

Communicating about your ADHD in the workplace doesn't have to be a formal revelation. Instead, you can subtly and effectively integrate it into your daily interactions.

- Sharing your strengths and challenges can foster a deeper understanding and support from your coworkers.
- For instance, you might casually mention how your ADHD fuels your creativity and ability to think quickly on your feet, which are assets to brainstorming sessions.
- At the same time, you could share strategies for managing time effectively or staying organized, such as setting digital reminders or using specific tools.
- This open communication demystifies ADHD and integrates it into the narrative of your professional persona as an array of unique strengths peppered with manageable challenges.

Lastly, building social capital is essential. You are involved in networking and are known as a reliable and positive force within your workplace.

- Ensure you deliver consistent results and meet your deadlines, as reliability can significantly boost your professional reputation.
- Engage positively with your colleagues, offer help when needed, and be a proactive part of solutions within your team.
- These actions help build a reservoir of goodwill and trust, making your daily work life smoother. They can also be invaluable during periods when you might need extra support or flexibility due to your ADHD.

Navigating professional relationships with ADHD involves a dynamic blend of showcasing your unique strengths, effectively managing your challenges, and actively engaging with your colleagues in a positive and supportive manner. By employing these strategies, you enhance your work experience and contribute positively to your workplace culture, making it more inclusive and diverse.

As we conclude this exploration into optimizing professional relationships, remember that the journey through the workplace is as much about personal growth as it is about professional development.

- Each interaction and project allows you to demonstrate your capabilities and forge deeper connections that enrich your professional life.
- In the next chapter, we'll explore strategies for effectively managing time and tasks, ensuring that you can harness your full potential in all aspects of your work life and turn everyday challenges into opportunities for success and satisfaction.

OPTIMIZING THE WORKPLACE WITH ADHD

As you step into your workspace each day, imagine it as a blank canvas, where you have the power to design an environment that not only boosts your productivity but also supports your unique needs as someone with ADHD. It's a place where each element, from your chair to the color of your walls, can be tailored to enhance focus, minimize distractions, and create a haven of efficiency. In this chapter, we'll explore how designing an ADHD-friendly workspace can transform your workday, making it less about struggling against your environment and more about thriving within it.

4.1 DESIGNING AN ADHD-FRIENDLY WORKSPACE

Ergonomic Setup for Focus

One of the first steps in optimizing your workspace is to ensure it is ergonomically supportive. This change will help you maintain focus while minimizing physical discomfort—a common distraction that can exacerbate ADHD symptoms.

- An ideal ergonomic setup includes adjustable seating that supports your back and encourages good posture, which can significantly affect your concentration ability.
- Consider a desk that can be adjusted for sitting and standing, allowing you to change your work position throughout the day.
- This variability can be particularly beneficial, as it reduces strain from prolonged sitting and provides a subtle change of pace that can help refresh your focus.
- Additionally, organize your desk layout so that essential tools are within easy reach, reducing the need to interrupt your workflow and risk getting sidetracked.

Strategic Organization

A strategically organized workspace can significantly reduce visual clutter, often a source of sensory overload for individuals with ADHD.

- Begin by categorizing your workspace into zones based on activities—have a designated area for computer work, another for reading or brainstorming, and a spot for personal items.
- Use drawer organizers or desktop trays to keep necessary documents and supplies neatly arranged and easy to find.
- Label these areas clearly if it helps you to remember their purposes.
- Having a place for everything makes it easier to focus on the task by keeping your physical space tidy and clear of mental clutter.

Personalization for Stimulus Control

Personalizing your workspace to control sensory stimuli is another key strategy.

- If noise is a frequent distraction, use noise-canceling headphones or a white noise machine to maintain your auditory focus.
- If you are sensitive to visual stimuli, position your desk away from high-traffic areas and use a simple, non-distracting background for your desktop wallpaper.
- Personal items like plants, photos, or a personal motivational quote can make your space feel more comforting and less sterile, subtly boosting your mood and productivity throughout the day.

Lighting and Color Psychology

Your workspace's lighting and color scheme can also significantly affect your concentration and motivation.

- Natural light is ideal; it reduces eye strain and enhances overall mood and energy levels.
- If natural light isn't an option, choose full-spectrum light bulbs that mimic the sun's natural rays.
- Regarding color, blue tones are known to have a calming effect and can enhance productivity, making them an excellent choice for wall colors or desktop backgrounds.
- Alternatively, if specific colors energize you or improve your focus, incorporating these into your workspace can create a personalized and conducive environment for your work needs.

By thoughtfully setting up your workspace to suit your ergonomic needs, strategically organizing your environment, personalizing your space to control stimuli, and using lighting and colors that enhance focus and mood, you create a setting that not only accommodates your ADHD but actively supports your best work. This tailored approach goes beyond mere functionality, crafting a space that resonates with your work style and psychological needs, transforming the daily grind into a more pleasant and productive experience.

4.2 NEGOTIATING ADHD ACCOMMODATIONS AT WORK

Navigating the workplace with ADHD often means you might need a few adjustments to perform at your best.

- Knowing your legal rights and communicating your needs can significantly improve getting your required support.
- Under laws like the Americans with Disabilities Act (ADA), you're entitled to reasonable accommodations that help mitigate the impact of disabilities, including ADHD, in the workplace.
- Reasonable accommodations mean a variety of modifications or adjustments to your job or work environment that enable you to perform your duties effectively.
- Understanding these rights is the first step toward advocating for yourself professionally.

When you're ready to discuss accommodations, how you communicate with your Human Resources (HR) department can significantly influence the outcome. It's essential to approach this conversation with clarity and preparedness.

- Before meeting with HR, gather documentation from your healthcare provider that outlines how ADHD affects your work and what accommodations could assist you.
- This preparation shows that you're serious and informed, which can help make the case that the accommodations are not just preferences but necessities.
- During the discussion, be clear and specific about what changes you need and why.
- For example, instead of saying you need a quieter space, explain how background noise disrupts your concentration and affects your productivity and propose potential solutions like noise-canceling headphones or a different workspace location.

Let's talk about what these accommodations might look like.

- Reasonable accommodations vary widely but often include things like flexible scheduling, which can allow you to work during hours when you feel most productive, or the option to work from home, reducing environmental distractions that might impede your focus.
- Other accommodations involve changes to information delivery; perhaps receiving written instructions along with verbal ones helps you process and retain the information better.
- Sometimes, taking short, frequent breaks throughout the day can significantly improve focus and productivity.
- These adjustments help create a work environment where you can thrive, showcasing your true capabilities without being hindered by your ADHD.

It is also crucial to maintain documentation of all communications about your accommodations.

- Keep records of submitted forms, emails exchanged, and meetings regarding your accommodation requests.
- This documentation can be invaluable not only for your records but also in instances where there might be misunderstandings or discrepancies in agreements.
- It ensures a clear trail of what accommodations were requested and approved, which can help maintain compliance and follow-up if accommodations still need to be implemented as agreed.

By understanding your legal rights, communicating effectively with HR, requesting reasonable accommodations, and keeping thorough documentation, you set the stage for a work environment that acknowledges and supports your unique needs. This proactive approach empowers you to advocate for your well-being and enhances your ability to perform effectively, contributing positively to your team and workplace.

4.3 TECHNIQUES FOR MINIMIZING DISTRACTIONS AND ENHANCING FOCUS

The distractions can sometimes seem overwhelming in the bustling rhythm of an office or even your home workspace.

- From the ping of a new email to the traffic of colleagues or family members around you, each distraction can feel like a slight tug away from your focus.
- For those with ADHD, these external distractions can be particularly disruptive, fragmenting our concentration and draining our productivity.

- Identifying these external distractions is one of the first steps to reclaiming your attention.
- Start by keeping a distraction log for a week.
- Note what interrupts your work, when it happens, and how it affects your focus.
- You might find patterns that weren't apparent before, like peak noisy hours in your office or certain notifications that consistently pull you away from tasks.

Once you've identified these distractions, implementing practical solutions can significantly reduce their impact.

- If noise is a frequent disruptor, consider setting up physical barriers such as privacy panels or noise-canceling headphones.
- Managing digital distractions involves more than self-control; technology can also assist here.
- Tools like website blockers can prevent you from drifting to non-work-related sites during focus times, and customizing notification settings on your devices can minimize unnecessary alerts.
- For instance, setting your phone and computer to 'Do Not Disturb' mode during critical work blocks can shield you from a barrage of pings that fragment your attention.

Internally, distractions are often just as challenging.

- These can include intrusive thoughts, physical restlessness, or fluctuating energy levels that pull your focus inward and away from work.
- Managing these internal distractions starts with mindfulness techniques.

- Mindfulness involves being present in the moment and observing your thoughts and feelings without judgment.
- Regular practice can help you recognize your mind wandering and gently guide it back to the task.
- Apps that offer guided mindfulness exercises can provide short sessions to fit into your workday to train your attention and enhance your focus.

Structured break times are another key strategy.

- The Pomodoro Technique, where you work intensively for 25 minutes, followed by a 5-minute break, can be incredibly effective.
- These short breaks allow you to rest your brain, reducing mental clutter and fatigue, which can exacerbate ADHD symptoms.
- During these breaks, engage in genuinely restorative activities rather than merely distractions—this might mean stepping away from all screens and taking a short walk, doing some stretches, or practicing deep breathing exercises.
- This intentional pausing can help reset your focus, making you more productive when you return to your tasks.

Creating personalized distraction management plans is essential for effectively navigating the workday with ADHD.

- Tailor plans to your specific triggers and effective coping mechanisms.
- Start by outlining what typically disrupts your focus and list the strategies you have found effective in managing these distractions.

- For example, you know that mid-afternoon is when you'll most likely lose focus. In that case, schedule your most demanding tasks in the morning and use the later hours for meetings or administrative tasks that require less intense concentration.

Focus-enhancing exercises can also play a crucial role in your daily routine.

- Physical activity can significantly boost cognitive function and focus, even in short bursts.
- Simple exercises like jumping jacks, a quick jog around your office, or even some yoga stretches can invigorate your body and sharpen your mind.
- Meditation, too, can be a powerful tool for enhancing focus.
- Regular practice can help calm an overactive mind, making it easier to concentrate on work tasks.
- Even just a few minutes of focused breathing or guided meditation can clear your head and improve your ability to concentrate throughout the day.

You create a robust framework that supports sustained concentration and productivity by combining these strategies — identifying and minimizing external distractions, using mindfulness to manage internal distractions, taking structured breaks, and incorporating focus-enhancing exercises. These techniques, tailored to your unique needs and work environment, can help you build a more focused and fulfilling workday, transforming how you engage with your tasks and manage your ADHD in a professional setting.

4.4 TIME MANAGEMENT TIPS FOR THE WORKPLACE

In the bustling environment of a modern workplace, managing your time becomes not just a skill but a necessity, especially when navigating the complexities of ADHD.

- Prioritizing tasks in a professional setting requires a more nuanced approach, as the immediacy of deadlines requires balance against the ever-changing priorities of corporate life.
- Extending the prioritization techniques discussed earlier, their application in a professional context often involves leveraging digital tools that enhance one's ability to manage multiple projects and responsibilities seamlessly.
- Platforms like **Asana** or **Microsoft To Do** can transform your workflow by allowing you to categorize tasks into projects, set priorities, and even delegate responsibilities without losing sight of the bigger picture.
- These tools often come with customizable notifications that help keep you on track without becoming a distraction, offering gentle reminders of upcoming deadlines or incomplete tasks.
- This digital approach helps keep your day structured. It visually represents your workload, which can be incredibly satisfying as you tick off completed tasks, giving a clear sense of accomplishment and progress.

Task batching is another transformative technique that suits the fast-paced nature of many professional environments and aligns well with the ADHD brain's operational style.

- The concept here is simple yet powerful: group and tackle similar tasks in designated time blocks.

- This method reduces the cognitive load and time lost in context switching, where shifting from one task to another can drain your mental energy and reduce efficiency.
- For instance, instead of responding to emails sporadically throughout the day, set a specific time to handle all your correspondence simultaneously.
- Similarly, if you need to create multiple presentations or reports, batching these tasks together can streamline your thought process and enhance focus.
- This approach makes handling individual tasks more manageable. It also segments your day into manageable chunks that make it easier to maintain focus, making it particularly effective for those with ADHD.

Setting professional boundaries around your time is crucial in ensuring these strategies work effectively.

- Strategies include having clear guidelines for meeting availability, responding to emails, and even informal chats.
- Communicate these boundaries clearly with your colleagues and supervisors.
- For instance, you might establish certain hours as 'deep work' periods during which you are unavailable for meetings or calls.
- These boundaries protect your most productive periods from interruption and signal to others that you value and manage your time effectively.
- Moreover, setting these boundaries and adhering to them can minimize feelings of stress and being overwhelmed, common challenges for individuals with ADHD, as it provides a structured framework within which to operate, reducing the anxiety associated with unpredictable workdays.

Regular time audits can provide insightful revelations into how you spend your workday.

- Track your activities for a period—say a week—and then analyze how you spent your time.
- Did unnecessary meetings bog you down?
- Did you spend too much time on a particular task?
- Are there tasks that could be delegated or streamlined?
- This exercise highlights areas to improve and helps reassess your workload and priorities.
- It can be eye-opening to see how much time certain tasks take compared to their importance to one's objectives.
- Armed with this information, you can make informed decisions about where to allocate your time more effectively, ensuring you align efforts with your professional goals and personal work style.
- This ongoing evaluation and adjustment process is key to developing a sustainable and productive work rhythm that supports your ADHD needs while fostering professional growth and satisfaction.

4.5 USING TECHNOLOGY TO BOOST WORKPLACE PRODUCTIVITY

In today's digital age, harnessing the right technology can be a game changer, especially for those managing ADHD. The right apps and digital tools can transform how we handle tasks, maintain focus, and organize our workflow. Imagine having a suite of tools specifically designed to cater to your ADHD-related challenges, enhancing your productivity without overwhelming you. Let's delve into some of these tools and how to integrate them effectively into your daily routine to maximize their benefits.

ADHD-friendly apps and tools are specifically designed to address the unique needs of individuals managing ADHD, focusing on enhancing productivity, focus, and task management.

- For instance, apps like **Forest** encourage focus by letting you grow a virtual tree that grows as you work and dies if you navigate to a distracting app. This app provides a fun and visually rewarding way to stay on task.
- Another invaluable tool is **Todoist**, which helps manage tasks through a user-friendly interface. It allows you to break projects into manageable tasks and set priorities and deadlines.
- These apps often include features like color-coding for organizing tasks by category or urgency, reminders to keep you on track, and progress tracking to represent your achievements visually.
- Incorporating these tools into your workflow can significantly enhance your ability to manage time and tasks effectively, turning potential chaos into a structured and manageable schedule.

Integrating these technologies seamlessly into your daily work-flows is crucial for maximizing their benefits.

- Begin by identifying the areas in your work life where you struggle the most — maintaining focus, keeping track of tasks, or managing your time.
- Once identified, select tools that address these specific challenges.
- For example, an app that blocks distracting websites during work hours could be beneficial if you find it hard to stay focused due to frequent interruptions.

- Integration means making these tools a part of your daily routine.
- Set aside some time to familiarize yourself with the functionalities of these apps.
- Customize their settings to suit your working style — for instance, setting up notifications for tasks that need starting or deadlines approaching.
- Making these tools a part of your everyday work life becomes second nature, supporting your productivity in intuitive and natural ways.

Evaluating new technologies is crucial to effectively ensuring they meet your ADHD-specific needs.

- When considering a new app or tool, look at its user interface first. Is it cluttered or intuitive?
- Tools designed with simplicity in mind are often better suited for ADHD, as they reduce cognitive load rather than adding to it.
- Check if the app allows customization. Can you adjust its settings to match your work style and preferences?
- Also, consider the app's ability to sync across devices.
- Consistency is crucial for managing ADHD effectively. Accessing your tasks and schedules across all your devices ensures you can stay on top of your work, whether at your desk or on the go.
- Lastly, look for reviews or feedback from other users with ADHD. Their insights can provide valuable information on the tool's performance in real-world scenarios, helping you make an informed decision.

Tech-based reminders and alerts are another aspect of these tools that can revolutionize how you manage your workload.

- Setting up effective reminders ensures that everything runs smoothly.
- Most task management apps allow you to set custom reminders for upcoming tasks or deadlines.
- Set a reminder an hour before a meeting or a day before a project deadline.
- These timely nudges can help keep you on track and reduce the anxiety of forgetting important tasks.
- Alerts can also be set up for regular breaks, encouraging you to step away from your desk, which can be crucial for maintaining mental clarity and preventing burnout.
- These small but powerful technological assists are like having a personal assistant in your pocket who understands the challenges of ADHD and supports your work accordingly.

By leveraging these ADHD-friendly apps and tools, integrating them effectively into your workflows, carefully evaluating new technologies, and setting up personalized reminders and alerts, you harness the power of technology to create a more productive, focused, and organized work environment. This proactive approach enhances your professional capabilities and empowers you to manage your ADHD confidently and efficiently.

As we wrap up this chapter, remember that the journey to optimizing your workplace with ADHD-friendly strategies is ongoing. The tools and techniques discussed here are not just about making your work easier; they're about transforming how you engage with your tasks, time, and talents. In the next chapter, we'll explore strategies for managing daily challenges, ensuring that every aspect of your work life aligns with your goals and needs, and helping you cope and thrive.

ORGANIZATIONAL MASTERY

Imagine walking into a space with everything arranged where you need it, where the chaos of clutter doesn't cloud your mind, and each item around you serves a functional or joyful purpose. For many with ADHD, this might sound like a distant dream, often overshadowed by the reality of scattered belongings and the daunting task of organizing them. Yet, the peace and efficiency of a well-organized space are within reach. This chapter is devoted to transforming that dream into your reality, providing you with decluttering techniques specifically tailored to the ADHD mind. These strategy designs don't just clean up your space but create environments that enhance focus, reduce stress, and maintain the serenity and functionality you need to thrive.

5.1 DECLUTTERING TECHNIQUES FOR THE ADHD MIND

Simplifying Decision-Making

One of the biggest hurdles during decluttering is often the decision-making process, which can feel overwhelming and exhausting.

- To combat this, introduce the "one-minute rule" into your routine.
- This simple yet effective strategy involves immediately dealing with any task or item that takes less than a minute to complete or put away.
- For example, if a book needs shelving or a jacket needs hanging, do it on the spot.
- This method drastically cuts down the pile of tasks or items that typically accumulate, often becoming daunting for anyone, particularly if you need help with decision paralysis.
- By handling these quick tasks immediately, you keep your space tidier and reduce the cognitive load, making the decision-making process more manageable and less stressful.

Categorization Strategies

When it comes to organizing, categorization is vital, especially for the ADHD mind, which can benefit from precise and logical groupings.

- Instead of merely organizing items by type, consider categorizing them by frequency of use.
- For instance, everyday items like your keys or wallet should have a designated spot that is easily accessible, preferably near the entrance of your home.
- Seasonal items, like holiday decorations or winter gear, can be stored in labeled bins in less accessible areas, such as the top shelf of a closet or the attic.
- This method of organization minimizes time spent searching for items and reduces frustration, making your daily routine smoother and more efficient.

Using Visual Reminders

For many with ADHD, visual cues are a powerful tool to maintain organization.

- Implementing a system of labels and color coding can significantly enhance your ability to locate and store items quickly.
- Use vibrant, contrasting colors to differentiate item categories, and label shelves, bins, and drawers clearly and boldly.
- Visual reminders can also extend to your scheduling; for instance, placing a whiteboard calendar in a central location to note important dates and tasks can help keep you on track.
- These visual systems help keep your physical space organized and provide a quick and clear reference that can help prevent overwhelm.

Regular Decluttering Schedule

Finally, establishing a regular decluttering schedule can prevent the task from becoming an overwhelming project that can only be tackled when it becomes unmanageable.

- Set aside a specific time each week or month, depending on your needs, to go through your space and clear out anything that isn't useful, necessary, or joy-sparking.
- Treat this scheduled time like an appointment, marking it as a recurring event on your calendar.
- Consistency is crucial; regularly maintaining the organization makes the process more routine and less daunting.
- This routine keeps your space functional and pleasant and reinforces the habit of decluttering, making it a natural part of your life rather than a dreaded chore.

Visual Element: Interactive Checklist

To aid in your decluttering efforts, consider using an interactive checklist. Here's a simple format you can adapt:

1. Daily Quick Cleans:

- Clear desk/workspace at the end of the day.
- Handle mail and packages as they arrive.

2. Weekly Sorting Tasks:

- Sort through and organize one drawer or shelf.
- Review and update the whiteboard calendar.

3. Monthly Deep Cleans:

- Check and declutter one specific area (e.g., closet, garage).
- Donate or dispose of items no longer needed.

This checklist can be printed or used as a digital reminder. It organizes and manages the decluttering process. It breaks down tasks into smaller, achievable actions that can significantly reduce the burden of maintaining an organized space.

Integrating these decluttering techniques into your life creates an environment that supports your daily needs and enhances your overall well-being. This design makes organization a feasible, sustainable part of your life, allowing you to focus more on living and less on the stress of clutter.

5.2 SYSTEMIZING YOUR DAY FOR PEAK EFFICIENCY

Creating a daily routine that complements the ADHD brain can be likened to setting the stage for a successful play, arranging each element to support the performance, or, in this case, your productivity and mental well-being.

- One effective strategy is to theme your days or dedicate specific time blocks to particular types of tasks.
- For instance, you might declare Monday your administrative day—dedicated to emails, scheduling, and planning—while Tuesday could focus on creative tasks such as brainstorming or content creation.
- This approach minimizes the cognitive load associated with task switching, a common challenge for those with ADHD.

- The brain appreciates this consistency; it thrives on knowing that time is set aside for every type of task, reducing anxiety and indecision about what to tackle next.

Moreover, structuring your day around themed tasks can help in harnessing the natural ebb and flow of your energy levels, which are often variable when you have ADHD.

- Recognizing and planning for these fluctuations can enhance your productivity.
- For example, if you know you're most energetic in the mornings, schedule your most demanding tasks and save the less intensive tasks for your lower-energy periods.
- It ensures that you work with your natural tendencies rather than against them. It also helps you maintain a steady pace throughout the day, reducing feelings of burnout and frustration.

Incorporating checklists and to-do lists into your daily routine is another cornerstone of effective day systemization.

- These tools are more than just reminders of tasks; they serve as external memory aids, crucial for navigating the forgetfulness that often accompanies ADHD.
- Start each day by writing down your tasks, breaking them down into clear, actionable steps.
- This breakdown makes the tasks seem more manageable and provides a clear roadmap of your day.
- As you check off each item, you track your progress and get a small boost of dopamine, the brain's reward neurotransmitter, which can be incredibly motivating for those with ADHD.

- To ensure these lists are effective, keep them visible. Post them on your fridge, use a desktop sticky note app, or carry a small notebook with you.
- The key is constant visibility, reinforcing your commitment to the tasks and reducing the likelihood of anything slipping through the cracks.

Setting clear and achievable goals for each day or week is equally important.

- Goals give you something concrete to work toward, providing a sense of direction and purpose.
- When setting these goals, make sure they are specific and measurable.
- A more practical goal than a vague one like "work on the project" would be "complete the first draft of the report."
- This specificity makes the goal more tangible and achievable, crucial for maintaining motivation.
- Furthermore, celebrate when you reach these goals.
- This celebration doesn't need to be elaborate. It can be as simple as a fifteen-minute break to do something you enjoy or treating yourself to your favorite snack.
- This positive reinforcement makes the journey toward your goals enjoyable and rewarding, fueling your motivation to continue.

Regular reflection and flexibility in adjusting your routines and strategies are crucial for long-term success.

- At the end of each week, take some time to reflect on what worked and what didn't.
- Ask yourself questions like, "Did I allocate enough time for

each task?" or "Were my daily themes effective in reducing task-switching fatigue?"

- This reflection helps you fine-tune your system for greater efficiency and encourages a mindset of continuous improvement.
- If a strategy isn't working, don't hesitate to tweak it or try something new.
- Flexibility is vital. As your life evolves, so should your strategies for managing it.
- This adaptive approach ensures that your systems remain practical and relevant, helping you meet current and future challenges with confidence and clarity.

5.3 THE ROLE OF ORGANIZATIONAL APPS IN MANAGING ADHD

In the digital age, apps have become indispensable tools for managing our daily lives, and they can be particularly transformative for those with ADHD.

- The right apps can act like an external brain, helping you organize thoughts, remember tasks, and track deadlines.
- However, not all apps are equal, especially when it comes to managing ADHD.
- It's crucial to select apps based on specific criteria that align with ADHD needs.
- User-friendliness is paramount; the app should have a clean, intuitive interface that doesn't require a steep learning curve, which can be a barrier to regular use.
- Customization options are also vital; the ability to tailor the app's functionalities to your specific preferences can significantly improve its effectiveness.

- For instance, setting multiple reminders for a single task or adjusting the visibility of tasks can help you manage your workflow more effectively.
- Moreover, integration capabilities enhance an app's utility manifold.
- An app that syncs with other tools like your digital calendar or email—can streamline your task management process, ensuring that all your information is consolidated and easily accessible.

When exploring the best organizational apps for ADHD, task managers like **Todoist** or **Asana** stand out due to their powerful organizing capabilities and user-friendly interfaces.

- These apps allow you to create tasks, categorize them, set priorities, and even delegate them if you work in a team.
- Reminder apps are also indispensable;
- **Due**, for instance, excels at sending nagging reminders until you can mark the task as completed, which is ideal for ADHD moments when you need just one more nudge to get things done.
- Note-taking apps like **Evernote** offer a versatile platform for storing all kinds of data, from typed notes to audio recordings and images, all of which can be tagged and searched easily.
- The common thread among these top apps is their ability to sync across devices. Syncing ensures that whether you're on your phone, tablet, or computer, your data is up-to-date and accessible, a crucial feature for seamlessly tracking your tasks and responsibilities.

Integrating these apps into your daily routine is vital to harness their full potential.

- Start by identifying which parts of your life need better organization — work tasks, household chores, or personal projects.
- Begin integrating the apps in these areas first.
- Consistency is key. To reinforce the habit, try using the apps at the same time each day, such as first thing in the morning or right before bed.
- Use notifications wisely. While they can be great reminders, too many can become overwhelming.
- Customize your notification settings to strike the right balance that keeps you informed but not stressed.
- Over time, these apps can become a natural part of your daily routine, significantly reducing the cognitive load of remembering every detail and allowing you more mental space to focus on the task.

Finally, while embracing the convenience of organizational apps, it's crucial to be mindful of privacy and data security, particularly when inputting personal or sensitive information.

- Opt for apps with strong encryption and clear, transparent privacy policies.
- Update your apps and passwords regularly to safeguard your data against breaches.
- Being proactive about security is not just about protecting your information; it's about ensuring your digital environment is as safe and supportive as your physical one.

By carefully selecting, integrating, and securing the right organizational apps, you can create a digital environment that significantly enhances your ability to manage the complexities of ADHD. These tools do more than just help you remember to do tasks; they empower you to master your responsibilities and free up your mind to engage more fully with life. As we close this chapter, remember that these apps are tools to serve you. They are part of a broader strategy designed to align your environment with your goals, helping you manage and thrive with ADHD.

As we progress, we'll explore coping mechanisms for daily challenges, building on the organizational strategies discussed here and ensuring you have a robust toolkit to manage every aspect of ADHD.

MAKE A DIFFERENCE WITH YOUR REVIEW

UNLOCK THE POWER OF GENEROSITY

"Small acts, when multiplied by millions of people, can transform the world."

— HOWARD ZINN.

People who give without expectation live longer, happier lives and make more money. So, if we've got a shot at that during our time together, darn it, I'm going to try.

To make that happen, I have a question for you...

Would you help someone you've never met, even if you never got credit for it?

Who is this person, you ask? They are like you—or, at least, like you used to be—less experienced, wanting to make a difference and needing help but not sure where to look.

Our mission is to make understanding and managing Adult ADHD accessible to everyone. Everything I do stems from that mission. And, the only way for me to accomplish that mission is by reaching...well...everyone.

This moment is where you come in. Most people judge a book by its cover (and its reviews). So here's my ask on behalf of a struggling adult with ADHD you've never met:

Please help that reader by leaving this book a review.

Your gift costs no money and takes less than 60 seconds to make real, but it can change a fellow reader's life forever. Your review could help…

…one more adult manage their ADHD and feel more in control. …one more person find peace amidst the chaos. …one more reader discover new strategies to improve their daily life. …one more individual realize they are not alone.

Simply scan the QR code below to leave your review:

If you feel good about helping a faceless reader, you are my kind of person. Welcome to the club. You're one of us.

I'm that much more excited to help you gain control over your day, find peace amidst the chaos, and master time management in a way that respects your neurodiversity. You'll love the tools and strategies I will share in the coming chapters.

Thank you from the bottom of my heart. Now, back to our regularly scheduled programming.

- Your biggest fan, Reese Hunter

COPING WITH DAILY CHALLENGES

Navigating the day-to-day with ADHD can often feel like you're an acrobat, balancing on a high wire while juggling multiple balls in the air. It's not just about avoiding the fall; it's about performing with grace under pressure despite the distractions and impulses pulling you in various directions. This chapter will equip you with strategies that help you maintain your balance and enable you to perform your daily routines with more control and less chaos. Here, we'll focus on managing one of the most common challenges: impulsivity. By understanding and mitigating impulsive behaviors, you create more space for thoughtful action, which is essential for achieving both short-term and long-term goals.

6.1 STRATEGIES FOR MANAGING IMPULSIVITY IN EVERYDAY LIFE

Identifying Impulsive Triggers

Impulsivity can often derail your plans, leading to unfinished tasks, rushed decisions, or strained relationships.

- The first step toward reigning in this impulsivity is recognizing what triggers it.
- These triggers can be emotional — like feeling stressed or overwhelmed — or situational, such as being in a high-energy environment.
- Begin by observing yourself and noting what circumstances or feelings precede impulsive decisions.
- Keep a journal of these observations; it can help you detect patterns and become more aware of when you're likely to act impulsively.
- Understanding your triggers is a powerful tool. It turns a seemingly spontaneous impulse into something predictable, giving you the upper hand in managing it.

Delay Tactics

Once you know your triggers, you can employ delay tactics, which help you pause before acting impulsively.

- One effective method is the 'pause-and-plan' approach.
- When you feel an urge to act impulsively, force yourself to take a mental step back.
- Give yourself a moment to consider the consequences of your actions.

- Ask yourself, "What will happen if I do this? Is there a better alternative?"
- This momentary pause can help you avoid regretful actions and make choices that align more closely with your goals.

Setting Physical Boundaries

The physical environment plays a significant role in managing impulsivity.

- If particular objects or settings trigger impulsive behavior, altering your environment can help control those impulses.
- For instance, if online shopping is a pitfall, try installing website blockers that limit your access to retail sites during vulnerable times.
- Similarly, if clutter in your workspace leads to distracted, impulsive task-switching, organize your space, creating a minimalist environment that promotes focus.
- By controlling your physical surroundings, you can steer your impulses more productively.

Mindfulness and Meditation

Mindfulness and meditation are not just buzzwords; they are practical tools that enhance your ability to control impulsivity.

- Mindfulness teaches you to be present in the moment, increasing your awareness of your thoughts and actions.
- It allows you to recognize the rise of impulsive urges without immediately acting on them.

- Conversely, meditation strengthens your self-regulation skills over time, making it easier to manage those urges.
- Start with short, daily sessions of meditation, using apps or guided videos if you find it difficult to practice alone.
- As your ability to focus improves, you likely notice a decrease in impulsive behaviors, leading to a calmer, more controlled approach to daily life.

Visual Aid: Mindfulness Exercise

Visualization Technique for Impulse Control

- Imagine a stop sign. Each time you recognize an impulsive urge, mentally visualize this stop sign.
- This image is a subliminal cue to pause and reflect, helping you make more deliberate decisions.
- Practice this technique regularly to turn it into a habitual response to impulsivity.

By implementing these strategies — identifying triggers, using delay tactics, setting physical boundaries, and practicing mindfulness and meditation — you can enhance your ability to manage impulsivity effectively. Each step in recognizing and controlling your impulses improves your daily interactions and tasks and contributes to your overall well-being and success in managing ADHD.

6.2 COPING WITH HYPERFOCUS: BALANCING PASSION AND OBLIGATIONS

Hyperfocus, a common phenomenon for many with ADHD, can feel like a superpower.

- It allows you to dive deeply into tasks or hobbies that interest you, often leading to high productivity and creativity.
- However, this intense concentration can sometimes become a double-edged sword.
- While it enables significant accomplishments in specific tasks, it can also lead to neglect of other important duties and responsibilities.
- Recognizing when you are entering a state of hyperfocus is crucial.
- You might notice that hours pass like minutes, and the world around you disappears.
- This focus might feel great when you're doing something you love, but it becomes problematic when it means forgetting to pick up your kids from school or neglecting other work responsibilities.

Setting timers and alarms is an effective strategy to manage your hyperfocus.

- By setting a strict time limit on activities that tend to lock in your attention, you ensure you don't spend too long on any one thing.
- For example, if you're working on a graphic design project or writing a report that you find particularly engaging, set a timer for one hour.

- When the timer goes off, it serves as a cue to step back and assess whether you should continue the task or move on to something else.
- This method helps balance tasks that ignite your passion and those that are necessary but less engaging.

Incorporating structured breaks into your routine is another vital aspect of managing hyperfocus.

- These breaks are intentional interruptions that can help you transition from one state of mind to another.
- Schedule these breaks at regular intervals, perhaps every hour or so, to step away from your work desk. Stretch, have a snack, or simply rest your mind.
- These pauses are not just physical breaks but mental ones, too.
- They allow you to reassess your priority list and make conscious decisions about how to proceed with your day.
- These structured pauses are necessary, or the entire day may pass without attending to other critical tasks or interacting with others.

Balancing your task list is perhaps one of the most challenging yet essential skills to master when dealing with hyperfocus.

- Plan your day to balance tasks requiring intense focus with less engaging ones.
- One effective method is to alternate between task types.
- For instance, after spending an hour on a high-focus task, switch to a low-focus task, such as responding to emails or organizing your workspace.
- Switching task levels prevents fatigue associated with

prolonged hyperfocus and ensures a more rounded completion of daily responsibilities.
- Additionally, visually organizing your tasks can be incredibly helpful.
- Use a planner or digital tool to categorize tasks by their demand level on your focus.
- Color-coding these tasks can quickly tell you the nature of each task and help you decide how to alternate them effectively.

Adopting these strategies creates a balanced approach to managing your day. While you capitalize on the periods of hyperfocus, you do not neglect other essential areas of your life. This balanced approach enhances productivity across various tasks and helps maintain relationships and personal well-being. Intense focus periods can sideline essential things you need for balance.

6.3 OVERCOMING PROCRASTINATION THROUGH MICRO-TASKING

Procrastination — the art of delaying or postponing tasks — is a familiar foe for many, particularly those managing ADHD.

- It often arises not from a lack of desire to complete tasks but from feeling overwhelmed by their scope or fearing that the result will not match expectations.
- Micro-tasking, the practice of breaking down a large task into small, manageable steps, emerges as a powerful strategy.
- Imagine facing the daunting task of organizing a year's worth of receipts for tax purposes.
- The mere thought might prompt procrastination.

- However, the task becomes less intimidating and more manageable by breaking it into smaller steps, such as sorting receipts by month, then by category, and finally entering them into a spreadsheet over several sessions.

The concept of Micro-tasking works by reducing the cognitive load associated with starting an overwhelming task.

- Each small step requires less mental effort and energy, making initiating and maintaining momentum easier.
- Once you begin and complete a few micro-tasks, your progress can motivate you to continue, creating a positive feedback loop that keeps procrastination at bay.
- There are several apps and tools designed to help you micro-task effectively.
- Apps like **Trello** allow you to create boards for different projects. Cards representing each micro-task can move from 'To Do' to 'Done', visually tracking your progress.
- Another helpful tool is **Microsoft To Do**, which lets you break tasks into subtasks and set reminders for each, ensuring that each step of the process is clearly defined and scheduled.

A personal reward system can significantly enhance the effectiveness of micro-tasking.

- This system involves setting up small rewards for completing each micro-task, which can help reinforce the behavior of working steadily through a list of tasks.
- For example, after sorting each month's receipts, you might reward yourself with a five-minute break, a small treat, or a short walk.

- These rewards provide positive reinforcement, making the task completion satisfying and enjoyable.
- It's important to align these rewards with your personal motivators.
- If social media is a typical distraction, use a five-minute social media check as a reward for completing a task.
- The reward is satisfying and keeps it within a controlled, productive context.

Accountability partnerships represent another layer of support in combating procrastination through micro-tasking.

- An accountability partner can be a friend, colleague, or even a coach who checks in with you regularly to monitor your progress on set tasks.
- These partnerships work on mutual commitment. You will likely follow through on tasks to satisfy someone you respect.
- Regular daily or weekly check-ins can provide external motivation to stay on course.
- During these check-ins, discuss what tasks you've completed, what's up next, and any challenges you're facing.
- This process keeps you accountable and provides an opportunity for feedback and encouragement, which can be crucial in maintaining momentum.

Implementing micro-tasking alongside these supportive strategies transforms overwhelming projects into small victories. This approach not only makes daunting tasks more accessible but also changes your overall relationship with work and productivity. Each small step completed punctuates your day with a sense of achievement, continuously motivating you toward the finish line without the weight of procrastination slowing you down.

6.4 MANAGING SENSORY OVERLOAD IN BUSY ENVIRONMENTS

In bustling environments, whether a crowded shopping mall, a busy office, or even a lively family gathering, the sensory input can sometimes feel like a deluge, overwhelming one's senses and scattering one's focus.

- For those with ADHD, who often experience heightened sensitivity to their surroundings, managing this sensory overload is crucial for maintaining composure and effectiveness.
- Recognizing what specific sensory inputs trigger your discomfort is the first critical step.
- It might be the cacophony of sounds in a crowded space, the harsh lighting of an office, or the cluttered space that makes you feel confined.
- Keeping a sensory diary where you note the environments and corresponding feelings can help you identify patterns and triggers.
- Understanding these can guide you in taking proactive steps to minimize exposure to these overwhelming stimuli.

The good news is that several tools and devices can help manage sensory input, ensuring you can maintain focus and stay composed even in sensorially challenging environments.

- Noise-canceling headphones are a fantastic investment for enjoying music and creating a bubble of calm in noisy settings.

- They can help you control auditory input, which, for many with ADHD, can be particularly distracting.
- Similarly, fidget devices such as stress balls or fidget spinners can offer a physical outlet for nervous energy and help maintain focus, especially during long periods of sitting or listening.
- These tools are not just functional; they control your interactions with your environment, empowering you to define how you experience and react to the world around you.

Creating sensory-friendly spaces, particularly in personal and professional environments where one spends a lot of time, can enhance one's ability to function and thrive.

- In your workspace, consider the lighting. Natural light is ideal, but if that's not possible, opt for lamps with soft, warm bulbs rather than harsh overhead lights.
- Organizing your space to reduce clutter can also help minimize visual stress.
- Use room dividers or privacy screens in open-plan offices to create a more defined and controlled workspace.
- You might designate a specific area at home as a sensory relaxation zone, with items that help soothe and calm, like soft blankets, relaxing music, or scented candles.
- These adjustments don't just make these spaces more comfortable. They actively support your productivity and well-being by reducing the sensory demands placed on you.

For immediate relief from sensory overload, several on-the-spot techniques can be lifesavers.

- Focused breathing exercises, where you concentrate solely on your breath, can help center your thoughts and calm your nervous system.
- Grounding exercises, which focus on the physical sensations of the objects around you, can also help anchor your senses in the present moment, diverting your attention from overwhelming stimuli.
- A brief session of guided meditation can also reset your sensory tolerance.
- Apps like **Headspace** or **Calm** offer short, guided meditation sessions you can do anywhere. These sessions can provide quick relief when you feel overwhelmed.

By employing these strategies, you gain valuable tools to manage sensory overload, allowing you to navigate busy environments more quickly and confidently. Whether through sensory tools, creating sensory-friendly spaces, or applying immediate relief techniques, you can control how you experience and interact with the world around you, turning potentially overwhelming situations into manageable encounters.

As we wrap up this exploration of daily challenges in Chapter 6, remember that managing ADHD is about more than just tackling difficulties; it's about enhancing your ability to navigate life's complexities with agility and insight. The strategies discussed here — from managing impulsivity and hyperfocus to overcoming procrastination and handling sensory overload — provide a toolkit for daily survival and thriving. As you continue to apply these strategies, you'll find yourself not only coping with the challenges

ADHD brings but also harnessing your unique capabilities for a fulfilling and productive life.

Looking ahead, Chapter 7 will delve into advanced decision-making techniques, helping you refine your ability to make informed, effective choices in both personal and professional realms. This next step will build on the skills you've developed here, ensuring you take on life's decisions confidently and clearly.

ADVANCED DECISION-MAKING TECHNIQUES

Picture this: you're at a bustling street food market, each stall offering delicious options. Where do you start? What do you choose? For someone with ADHD, everyday decisions can often feel just as overwhelming as choosing from a myriad of culinary delights. But what if there was a tool that could simplify these choices, making decision-making less daunting and more straightforward? Enter the decision matrix, a visual tool that can transform complex decisions into clearer, more manageable ones. This chapter delves into how you can use decision matrices to streamline your decision-making process, ensuring that choices no longer stall your progress but propel you forward.

7.1 USING DECISION MATRICES TO SIMPLIFY CHOICES

Introduction to Decision Matrices

A decision matrix is a table used to evaluate and prioritize a list of options based on specific, predefined criteria.

- Think of it as creating a mini "competition" among your choices, where each contender scores on aspects that are important to you.
- This method is particularly effective for visual thinkers and those who benefit from structured frameworks — traits commonly found in individuals with ADHD.
- A decision matrix lays out your options and criteria, helping remove ambiguity from decisions and making it easier to see which choice best aligns with your objectives.

Designing a Custom Matrix for ADHD

Creating your decision matrix might sound complex, but it's pretty straightforward. Begin by listing your options as rows on a table and the criteria you want to use to judge these options as columns.

- For example, if you decide on a new project management tool, your criteria include cost, ease of use, compatibility with existing systems, and customer support.
- Next, assign a weight to each criterion based on its importance to you. This step is crucial because it helps quantify what matters most in your decision-making process.

- Now, score each option against each criterion on a scale (1 to 5). Multiply these scores by the weights of your criteria and sum them up to get a total score for each option.
- The option with the highest score will be your best choice according to your criteria and weights.

Case Study

Consider the case of Alex, a freelance graphic designer with ADHD, who used a decision matrix to decide which software subscription to purchase.

1. Alex's criteria included cost, features, user interface, and customer reviews.
2. By weighting these factors according to personal priorities and scoring each software option accordingly, the decision matrix clarified that the initially more expensive software was the best choice due to its superior features and user interface.
3. This method simplified what seemed like an overwhelming decision and ensured that the choice aligned with Alex's specific needs and preferences.

Matrix Adaptations for Different Contexts

While the basic format of a decision matrix is quite universal, its flexibility allows for adaptations to suit different contexts.

- If you're making a personal decision, such as choosing a new car, your criteria might be more subjective, such as aesthetic appeal or driving comfort. In professional contexts, criteria are often more data-driven, like ROI or alignment with strategic goals.

- You can also adapt the matrix to manage daily decisions by simplifying the requirements and scoring system, making it a quick and effective tool for smaller, routine choices.
- This adaptability makes the decision matrix a versatile tool in your decision-making arsenal, tailored to meet diverse needs and contexts.

By incorporating decision matrices into your decision-making process, you equip yourself with a powerful tool that clarifies and simplifies choices. Whether you're facing major life decisions or everyday selections, this tool helps you approach each confidently and clearly, ensuring that your choices are well-considered and aligned with your goals. As you continue to apply and refine this technique, you'll find that making decisions becomes a less stressful and more empowering part of your life.

7.2 MINIMIZING DECISION FATIGUE WITH ROUTINE BUILDING

Imagine juggling multiple balls, each representing a decision you must make — from what to wear to what to eat to how to prioritize your work tasks.

- For someone with ADHD, this juggling act isn't just a morning routine; it's a constant, day-long endeavor.
- This challenge is where understanding and managing decision fatigue becomes crucial. Decision fatigue refers to the deteriorating quality of decisions an individual makes after a lengthy decision-making session.
- For individuals with ADHD, who often experience quicker depletion of decision-making energy, this can lead to suboptimal choices and increased stress.

- However, by establishing well-structured routines, you can significantly reduce the number of decisions you need to make, preserving your mental energy for those decisions that truly matter.

Think of routine as your personal assistant, taking over the mundane decision-making processes that eat up your cognitive reserves.

- By automating daily decisions, routines free up your mental space, allowing you to focus on higher priorities.
- For instance, consider the impact of having a fixed morning routine: waking up at the same time, following a set sequence of activities — perhaps meditating, then showering, followed by breakfast.
- This structured start can dramatically reduce the number of decisions you must make, setting a calm, controlled tone for the day.
- Similarly, having a predetermined menu can prevent the mental drain of deciding what to eat each time.
- This menu doesn't mean every meal needs to be the same, but having a weekly meal plan reduces the frequency and effort of meal-related decisions.

Let's delve deeper into how routines can transform your daily life.

- Take the example of wardrobe management — a common source of decision fatigue.
- You can eliminate morning indecision by organizing your clothing into sets or deciding your outfits the night before.
- This approach saves time and reduces the cognitive load, allowing you to preserve mental energy for creative or critical work tasks.

- Another effective routine involves scheduling specific blocks of time to check emails or messages.
- Instead of constantly reacting to every notification, designate two or three periods throughout the day for this task.
- This routine helps manage your focus and productivity and reduces the stress of feeling like you need to be perpetually available.

Supporting these routines with the right tools can further enhance their effectiveness. Various apps and software designs help you build and maintain routines.

- For example, reminder apps can prompt you about the different phases of your daily routine, ensuring you don't skip or forget any steps.
- Scheduling software can be invaluable, especially for managing complex tasks and appointments. These tools often offer customizable features, allowing you to set up notifications and reminders that best suit your workflow.
- Habit-tracking apps are another fantastic resource. They help you monitor your progress in establishing new routines, providing insights into what's working and what needs adjustment. Reviewing these insights lets you fine-tune your routines, ensuring they align with your evolving needs and preferences.

Incorporating these strategies into your life isn't just about reducing the number of decisions you make. It's about making each day more manageable and less overwhelming. By understanding the impact of decision fatigue and using routines to mitigate it, you empower yourself to focus more on what truly matters, enhancing your productivity and overall quality of life. As you refine these routines, remember that the goal is to support your journey naturally and sustainably, allowing you to navigate your day with confidence and energy.

7.3 STRATEGIES FOR LONG-TERM PLANNING WITH ADHD

Long-term planning can often feel like you're trying to read a map in the dark when you have ADHD.

- The challenges are real — focusing on distant goals when immediate tasks demand your attention or managing the complexities of a project that spans months or even years.
- These tasks require sustained attention and detailed, step-by-step processing, which can be particularly taxing if your ADHD symptoms include distractibility or difficulty with time management.
- Recognizing these challenges is the first step in overcoming them, allowing you to approach long-term planning with strategies that play to your strengths.

Understanding that traditional goal-setting frameworks might not always align with how your ADHD brain works is crucial.

Though the S.M.A.R.T. goals — **S**pecific, **M**easurable, **A**chievable, **R**elevant, and **T**ime-bound, are important — the model can require adaptation to suit your needs better.

- For instance, the 'achievable' aspect might need to be more flexible, acknowledging that, on some days, your ADHD might significantly impact what you can accomplish.
- Similarly, 'time-bound' can be a stressor if interpreted too

rigidly, as the fluctuating nature of ADHD can make some days more productive than others.

- To adapt S.M.A.R.T. goals, you might set ranges instead of fixed targets or allow goalposts to shift as you better understand your capacity and resources over time.
- This flexibility can prevent feelings of frustration or failure, which are often counterproductive.

Visual planning tools can transform abstract goals into tangible, manageable parts, making them less overwhelming and more engaging.

- Gantt charts, for example, provide a visual timeline for your project, breaking down larger goals into smaller, sequential tasks.
- This tool can help you visualize the entire scope of a project at a glance, from start to finish, making it easier to track progress and adjust timelines as needed.
- Mind maps are another fantastic tool, especially during the brainstorming phase of planning.
- They allow you to visually organize information, connecting ideas and tasks in a non-linear format, which can align with the ADHD thinking style.
- Vision boards can also serve as a daily visual reminder of your goals, keeping them front and center in a motivating and inspiring way.

Regular review and adjustment sessions are essential when it comes to long-term planning with ADHD.

- These sessions provide opportunities to check your progress, reflect on what's working or not, and adjust your plans as needed.

- This check could be as simple as a monthly sit-down with your planner or a more formal review with mentors or colleagues.
- During these reviews, ask yourself:

  - Are the goals still relevant?
  - Have circumstances changed that require a shift in strategy?
  - Are there new tools or resources that could make achieving your goals easier?

- Keeping this feedback loop active ensures that your plans are living documents, adaptable, and responsive to your changing needs and situations. It also helps maintain motivation, as regular reviews allow you to see and celebrate your progress, which can be incredibly encouraging.

Implementing these strategies for long-term planning acknowledges the unique challenges posed by ADHD and leverages your strengths. By adapting goal-setting frameworks to be more flexible, using visual tools to clarify and manage your plans, and maintaining a routine of regular review and adjustment, you can transform long-term planning from a source of stress to a structured, manageable process that moves you toward your aspirations. Whether planning a career move, a large personal project, or anything in between, these strategies provide a roadmap that respects your neurodiversity and empowers you to succeed on your terms.

7.4 COGNITIVE REMEDIATION TECHNIQUES TO ENHANCE DECISION-MAKING SKILLS

Cognitive remediation might sound like a complex term reserved for neuroscientists. Still, it's a practical approach you can integrate into your daily life to boost your decision-making skills. Essentially, cognitive remediation involves exercises and practices designed to improve mental functions, which can be particularly beneficial for individuals with ADHD who might struggle with aspects of decision-making such as impulsivity, maintaining focus, or effectively weighing different options. Refining these cognitive skills can enhance your decision-making ability more strategically and clearly.

Let's delve into some techniques that can help boost cognitive flexibility, an essential skill that allows you to think about multiple concepts or consider various perspectives simultaneously.

- This technique is crucial in decision-making, enabling you to evaluate various options and outcomes without becoming fixated on a single track.
- Brain training games are a fun and effective way to improve this skill.
- These games often require you to think on your feet and adapt quickly to new information, mirroring the rapid decision-making scenarios you might face in daily life.
- Additionally, engaging in problem-solving exercises that challenge you to find solutions under time constraints can simulate real-life decision-making pressures, helping you practice maintaining calm and focus during stressful situations.
- Another powerful approach is targeted cognitive behavioral therapy (CBT) exercises, which can help you

recognize and modify unhelpful thought patterns or decision-making habits, fostering a more flexible and adaptive mindset.

Enhancing your working memory is another critical area that can significantly impact your decision-making abilities.

- Working memory is crucial for keeping information active in the mind, manipulating it, and using it in thinking processes, all critical steps in making informed decisions.
- To strengthen this aspect of cognitive function, you can use memory exercises, like repeating lists of numbers or complex sequences, which train your brain to retain and process information more effectively.
- Mnemonic devices, acronyms, or visualizing stories to remember details can be practical tools to enhance memory retention.
- Furthermore, the digital age offers many apps designed to improve memory and cognitive skills through structured exercises that you practice regularly.

Incorporating feedback loops into your decision-making process is a transformative strategy involving reflecting on your decisions, analyzing the outcomes, and using this information to refine your approach in future scenarios.

- This practice encourages a mindset of continuous improvement, which is essential for adapting and thriving in an ever-changing environment.
- By consistently applying these feedback loops, you create a dynamic learning experience where each decision, regardless of its success or failure, contributes to your developing expertise.

By integrating these cognitive remediation techniques into your routine, you equip yourself with tools to enhance your decision-making skills.

- These practices prepare you to handle complex decisions more effectively, contributing to greater confidence and reduced anxiety when making choices.
- They foster a brain environment ripe for growth and improvement, ensuring that your decision-making skills evolve continuously to meet the demands of daily life and the challenges of managing ADHD.

As we wrap up this exploration of advanced decision-making techniques, remember that the journey to enhanced cognitive skills is ongoing and cumulative. Each step you take builds upon the last, gradually crafting a sharper, more agile mind that can navigate the complexities of life with ADHD with greater ease. The next chapter will focus on leveraging technology and tools to enhance these cognitive strategies further, providing practical applications and resources to support your continuing growth.

LEVERAGING TECHNOLOGY AND TOOLS

In a world that considers technology and apps as distractions, imagine turning the tide and using these tools as lifelines to navigate the bustling currents of life with ADHD. In this chapter, we're diving into the digital toolbox to uncover time management apps designed to work with your unique brain wiring. Not just about ticking off tasks, these apps can be necessary allies, transforming the overwhelming waves of responsibilities into a manageable flow and enhancing your productivity and peace of mind.

8.1 REVIEWING THE BEST APPS FOR TIME MANAGEMENT

Navigating the digital landscape can be overwhelming, with countless apps promising to boost your productivity and manage your time. Yet, not all apps are equal, especially when it comes to meeting the specific needs of individuals with ADHD. Let's explore some of the leading apps that have been making waves for their effectiveness in managing time, particularly for those with ADHD - **Trello**, **Asana**, and **Todoist**.

Trello is renowned for its visually intuitive interface. It organizes tasks using boards, lists, and cards.

- This visual setup is ideal if you find traditional to-do lists challenging.
- You can create different boards for various projects, and lists can represent different phases or types of tasks within each board.
- Each card can be moved from one list to another, mimicking the progress of a task from initiation to completion.
- This movement provides a satisfying visual cue of progress and helps keep track of multiple tasks without feeling overwhelmed.

Asana takes project management a notch higher by offering more detailed task management features.

- It allows you to assign tasks to specific dates and collaborators, making it perfect for a team environment.
- The ability to break tasks into subtasks allows you to manage complex projects by dividing them into manageable units. This technique can be particularly beneficial if you break down tasks to combat ADHD-driven procrastination.
- The timeline view connects your tasks on a visual timeline, helping you see the bigger picture and understand how tasks align with project deadlines.

Todoist offers a clean and straightforward interface that helps you manage tasks efficiently.

- It allows you to set priority levels for each task, which can help you manage your day by focusing on what truly needs immediate attention.
- The recurring tasks feature is handy.
- It automatically reminds you of daily, weekly, or monthly tasks, which can be a boon if remembering regular tasks is challenging.

Customizing these apps to suit your ADHD better can significantly enhance their efficacy.

- For instance, setting repetitive reminders can prevent tasks from slipping through the cracks, a common issue when juggling multiple responsibilities.
- Color-coding tasks based on priority or type of activity can also provide visual cues that help you assess your task list quickly.
- Integrating these apps with other digital tools, such as calendar apps or digital notebooks, can create a cohesive system of reminders and notes that keep you organized and on track.

User experiences and ratings often show how these apps perform in real-life scenarios, especially for those with ADHD.

- Many users appreciate these apps' flexibility and customization options, stating that they help significantly reduce the anxiety associated with time management.
- However, it's important to remember that each person's

experience is unique, and what works for one might not work for another.

- Therefore, exploring these apps through trial and error is essential, keeping your specific needs in mind.

Integrating these apps into your daily routine is crucial for reaping their full benefits.

- Start by setting aside some time to familiarize yourself with the features of each app.
- Then, gradually begin integrating them into your daily planning.
- Set reminders to check these apps regularly throughout the day, which can help make their usage a habit rather than a sporadic attempt at organization.

By embracing these digital tools, you arm yourself with more than just apps; you equip yourself with strategies that transform how you interact with time, tasks, and productivity. Whether visualizing tasks on **Trello**, breaking down projects on **Asana**, or prioritizing daily activities on **Todoist**, these tools offer more than just convenience. They offer a new way to harness your strengths and navigate the challenges of ADHD with confidence and creativity.

8.2 GADGETS THAT HELP MAINTAIN FOCUS AND REDUCE STRESS

Imagine your daily routine enhanced not just by apps and strategies but also by physical gadgets explicitly designed to align with your needs, especially if you have ADHD. These are not just tools; they're your partners in navigating the complexities of maintaining focus and managing stress, tailored to provide support where it's most needed. Let's explore some innovative gadgets that can transform how you interact with your environment, ensuring you remain focused and stress-free at work or home.

Wearable technology like smartwatches and fitness trackers has revolutionized how we interact with our health and time. For someone with ADHD, these devices are more than just fitness tools; they are personal assistants strapped to your wrist.

- Consider a smartwatch that tracks your steps and heart rate and helps you manage your time and tasks.
- These watches can vibrate gently to remind you of appointments or when it's time to switch tasks, effectively keeping you on track without the disruptive buzz of a loud alarm.
- Moreover, many fitness trackers now come with stress management features. These features monitor heart rate variability to indicate stress levels and suggest activities like breathing exercises when stress spikes.
- This real-time feedback can be invaluable in helping you manage your ADHD symptoms. It provides alerts that help you take a break or refocus before you feel overwhelmed.

Regarding reducing stress, some gadgets create a calming atmosphere wherever you are.

- Wearable stress trackers, for instance, measure physiological signals such as heart rate and skin temperature to gauge your stress levels, providing feedback that helps you recognize stress responses.
- Some of these gadgets pair with apps that offer guided relaxation techniques, helping you calm down in stressful situations.

- Additionally, consider devices that promote relaxation through sensory stimulation, such as handheld massagers or electric aroma diffusers that fill your space with calming scents.
- These gadgets can be especially beneficial if you experience sensory overload, as they can soothe your senses and reduce anxiety.

Focusing in a noisy or busy environment can be a significant hurdle if you have ADHD.

- Noise-canceling headphones are a fantastic solution. They help block out distracting background noise and allow you to concentrate on the task.
- These headphones can be used with calming soundtracks or white noise, enhancing your ability to focus, especially in open office environments or busy homes.
- Similarly, electronic fidget devices can offer a way to channel excess energy without disrupting your focus.
- Unlike traditional fidget spinners, these electronic gadgets often feature various textures and buttons to subtly engage your senses, providing a tactile outlet for your energy that helps maintain concentration.

Ergonomic devices are crucial for maintaining focus and physical health for those who spend long hours at a desk.

- Specialized ergonomic keyboards and mouse devices reduce strain on your hands and wrists, preventing fatigue and discomfort.
- These devices keep your body in a more natural position, helping you maintain focus for extended periods.

- Posture correctors or ergonomic chairs can also make a significant difference. They ensure you're seated comfortably and correctly, reducing the physical distractions that can lead to loss of focus.
- Consider a standing desk converter, which allows you to alternate between sitting and standing while working.
- This change in posture can help alleviate physical stiffness and increase blood flow, enhancing your alertness and focus.

Integrating these gadgets into your daily life can significantly enhance your ability to manage ADHD symptoms, helping you maintain focus and reduce stress. Whether through wearable tech that keeps you on schedule, devices that calm your senses, or ergonomic solutions that enhance your physical comfort, each gadget offers a unique benefit that can make your day smoother and more productive. By choosing the right combination of these tools, you can create an environment supporting your work and well-being, turning daily challenges into opportunities for success and satisfaction.

8.3 HOW TO USE TECH FOR MINDFULNESS AND RELAXATION

In the constant hustle and the endless to-do lists, finding moments of calm and clarity feels like a luxury you can't afford. However, even those bustling moments can transform into islands of tranquility and focus with the right tools.

Mindfulness apps like **Headspace**, **Calm**, and **Insight Timer** are not just phone applications; they are gateways to mental clarity and stress reduction, specially tailored to help you navigate the challenges of ADHD.

- **Headspace** offers a user-friendly interface and a variety of guided meditations that focus on different aspects of mindfulness, such as concentration, relaxation, or specific issues like anxiety or sleep. These guided sessions gently lead you through mindfulness exercises, making meditation accessible, especially if you're new to the practice or struggle to concentrate.
- **Calm** also provides a wide range of meditation options. Still, it's mainly known for its sleep stories and calming soundscapes, which can be incredibly beneficial if you struggle with ADHD-related insomnia or restlessness.
- **Insight Timer** features the most extensive free library of meditations, with thousands of sessions available. What makes it especially suitable for ADHD is the ability to filter sessions by duration, allowing you to find short meditations that fit into a busy schedule or longer sessions for more profound relaxation.
- These apps not only help improve focus and reduce stress but also teach valuable skills in managing ADHD symptoms, such as dealing with impulsivity or emotional dysregulation.

Transitioning into virtual reality (VR), this technology uniquely enhances your relaxation routines by creating immersive environments that can transport you away from the chaos of daily life.

- Imagine slipping on a VR headset and finding yourself on a peaceful beach, listening to the waves and feeling as though you're miles away from any stressor.
- VR setups can be particularly effective for sensory relaxation and mental decluttering, providing a fully immersive experience that traditional meditation apps can't achieve.

- These VR environments can be customized to your preferences, whether you find solace in a quiet forest, a serene beach, or even a distant planet, making relaxation an engaging and highly personal experience.

Wearable technology also plays a vital role in managing stress and enhancing relaxation.

- Devices that use biofeedback allow you to monitor and control physiological functions, such as breathing and heart rate, which are often affected by stress.
- By giving you real-time feedback, these devices enable you to recognize your stress responses and learn to control them more effectively, using techniques like paced breathing or mindfulness.
- This immediate feedback is invaluable in helping you understand your body's signals and how to manage them, making stress management more intuitive and effective.

Integrating these technologies into your daily routine can maximize their benefits and help you maintain a consistent relaxation and mindfulness practice.

- Setting specific times for meditation or relaxation sessions, such as during a morning routine or right before bed, can help make these practices a regular part of your day.
- Additionally, using reminders or scheduling features on your phone or smart device can keep you accountable and ensure you take those much-needed breaks to clear your mind and reduce stress.

By embracing these mindfulness tools and integrating them into your life, you open up a new path toward managing ADHD with greater ease and effectiveness. Whether through quick meditation sessions with an app, immersive relaxation experiences with VR, or learning to control your stress responses with wearable technology, these tools offer practical and accessible solutions to enhance your mental well-being and improve your overall quality of life.

8.4 SETTING UP NOTIFICATION SYSTEMS FOR ADHD MANAGEMENT

Imagine a world where you set your smartphone to catch your attention and genuinely enhance your productivity and peace of mind instead of being interrupted by every beep, buzz, and blink of your device.

- For those navigating life with ADHD, properly managing notifications can transform our devices from sources of distraction into powerful allies.
- Customizing smartphone notifications is more than just turning off unnecessary alerts; it involves strategically setting up reminders and alerts that ensure essential tasks don't slip through the cracks while avoiding sensory overload.

You can start by diving into the settings of your smartphone to customize which notifications you receive and how they alert you.

- For instance, most phones allow you to set up VIP lists for your email app, ensuring that messages from key contacts trigger alerts, while less critical emails remain silent until you choose to check them.

- This prioritization can be particularly useful in maintaining focus during work hours or dedicated family time, as it filters out the noise, allowing only crucial communications to come through.

Prioritizing app notifications is another crucial step.

- Evaluate which apps you need immediate notifications from and adjust their settings accordingly.
- For example, your calendar app alerts might be essential for keeping you on schedule.
- In contrast, notifications from a social media app might be less urgent and can, therefore, be muted during work hours.
- Many apps also offer customization within their settings, allowing you to choose the type of notifications you receive, such as sounds, badges, or banners.
- Opt for subtle notifications like badges for less urgent apps to reduce distractions without missing out on important updates.

Smart home assistants, such as **Google Home** or **Amazon Alexa**, extend this customization into your living space, offering a hands-free way to stay on top of your tasks.

- These devices can set reminders and timers and even control smart home devices, which can help create an environment with fewer distractions.
- For instance, you can use voice commands to set a reminder for your next appointment or start a work session timer.
- You can also integrate these assistants with smart home gadgets to control lighting, temperature, and noise levels,

creating an optimal environment for concentration or relaxation without stopping what you're doing.

Email management tools and plugins significantly streamline how you handle your inbox, which can be a source of endless distractions.

Tools like **Boomerang for Gmail or Outlook** help you schedule emails to send later, set follow-up reminders, and even pause your inbox, allowing you to control when and how you deal with email.

- These tools can filter important emails and set priority alerts, ensuring no critical communications are lost in the clutter.
- By managing your email more efficiently, you can spend less time sorting through your inbox and focusing more on tasks that require your attention.

Integrating these systems can create a comprehensive management system that keeps you informed and organized without stress.

- For instance, syncing your smartphone alerts with your computer and smartwatch ensures you're up to date on your schedule and tasks, regardless of your device.
- Include syncing calendar events across all devices, setting location-based reminders on your phone and smartwatch as soon as you reach a specific place, or even having your smart home assistant remind you of your to-dos when you arrive home.

By setting up a personalized and integrated notification system, you harness the power of technology to cater to your unique needs, making life with ADHD manageable and more enjoyable and productive. Whether through customizing app notifications, utilizing smart home assistants, managing your emails more effectively, or syncing all your devices, the proper setup can give you a sense of control and calm, helping you focus on what truly matters.

8.5 USING SOCIAL MEDIA WISELY WITH ADHD

Navigating the vibrant and ever-evolving landscape of social media can be particularly challenging when you're managing ADHD. The endless stream of updates, notifications, and multimedia content can easily lead to overstimulation and time mismanagement. However, with a few strategic adjustments, social media can become a tool that enhances rather than hinders your daily life, personally and professionally.

- The lure of social media lies in its ability to keep us connected and informed, but for someone with ADHD, the constant influx of information can be overwhelming.
- It's easy to fall into the rabbit hole of endless scrolling, where minutes turn into hours without much to show.
- This challenge is not just about willpower; the design of these platforms exploits our brain's desire for novelty and immediate gratification, which can be particularly enticing for the ADHD mind.
- Recognizing this distraction is crucial to approaching social media with strategies that align with your goals and ADHD management plans.

One effective strategy is setting specific times for social media use to help contain potential distractions.

- Consider limiting your social media activity to certain times of the day that are less disruptive to your productivity.
- For instance, checking social media during a lunch break or after completing a significant task can minimize the impact on your work or personal tasks.
- It's also helpful to use features like **Do Not Disturb** or **Focus Mode** on your devices during work hours or family time, which can help you stay present in the moment without the constant pings pulling your attention away.

Moreover, curating your social media feeds can significantly reduce stress and enhance your online experience.

- Start by unfollowing or muting accounts that trigger stress or are irrelevant to your interests.
- This change declutters your feed and ensures that the content you see is uplifting or beneficial.
- Make it a habit to actively follow and engage with accounts that inspire or align with your professional interests.
- This realignment can transform your social media platforms into sources of inspiration and networking opportunities rather than sources of distraction.

However, even the best plans can only succeed with the right tools to support them. Tools and apps to manage and limit social media use can be invaluable.

- Apps like **Freedom** or **StayFocusd** allow you to block distracting websites or apps during designated times, helping you stay on track with your daily goals.

- These tools can be customized to your schedule, allowing you to choose whether you need more or less access to social media, depending on the demands of your day.

Creating a healthy online environment also involves being mindful of how social media interactions affect your emotional well-being.

- Social media can sometimes be a battleground of opinions and negativity, which can be particularly draining if you're sensitive to conflict or criticism, a common trait among those with ADHD.
- Engaging in positive communities online, whether through groups that share your interests or professional networks, can provide support and constructive interaction.
- Remember, the mute and block functions are there for a reason—don't hesitate to use them to protect your mental space.

By setting boundaries, curating your feed, utilizing management tools, and choosing positive interactions, you can tailor your social media use to serve you better. This approach not only helps in managing your ADHD but also turns social media into a resource that supports your goals and enriches your life rather than a distraction that drains your time and energy.

8.6 EDUCATIONAL TOOLS FOR LEARNING AND SKILL DEVELOPMENT

When it comes to learning new skills or deepening existing knowledge, the traditional one-size-fits-all approach often falls short for those with ADHD. The good news is that the digital age has brought many educational tools and platforms that cater specifically to diverse learning styles, particularly benefiting those with ADHD. These resources transform learning from a static, often frustrating activity into a dynamic and engaging process that plays to the strengths of individuals with ADHD, such as their ability to hyperfocus on areas of interest and their need for interactive content.

Platforms like **Khan Academy**, **Coursera**, and **Lynda** offer a range of educational content that covers everything from academic subjects to professional skills development. What sets these platforms apart is their ability to provide interactive, self-paced learning experiences ideal for ADHD learners.

- For instance, **Khan Academy** offers practice exercises and instructional videos that allow learners to control the pace of their education, revisiting complex topics as needed, which can be crucial for mastering challenging material.
- **Coursera** and **Lynda (now LinkedIn Learning)** provide professional courses, including video lectures, quizzes, and hands-on projects. These help retain information and engage different cognitive skills, making learning more comprehensive and enjoyable.

The incorporation of multimedia learning tools is a game-changer for ADHD learners.

- Video tutorials, for example, combine auditory and visual learning, making complex information more accessible and easier to digest.
- Platforms like **YouTube** have countless educational channels that summarize topics with visuals and real-life

examples, catering to the ADHD preference for dynamic and contextual learning.

- Interactive simulations on sites like **PhET Interactive Simulations** offer hands-on experiences in physics, biology, and chemistry. They allow learners to see the immediate effects of their actions in the simulation, enhancing their understanding and retention of complex concepts.

For those looking to advance their professional skills in a manner that aligns with ADHD learning needs, online courses and programs from platforms like **Udemy** and **Pluralsight** are invaluable.

- These platforms offer courses from software development to creative arts, many taught by industry professionals.
- The design of these courses caters to learners at different levels, from beginners to advanced, and includes community forums where students can interact with peers and instructors.
- The additional layer of support and interaction can enhance learning for someone with ADHD.

Feedback and progress tracking are critical components of effective learning, especially for ADHD learners who benefit from regular reinforcement and recognition of their progress.

- Most educational platforms provide some form of feedback, whether through automated quizzes, instructor assessments, or peer reviews, which helps learners understand where they stand and what areas need improvement.

- Additionally, these platforms often have dashboards that track course progress and achievements, such as badges or certificates, which are visual reminders of accomplishments and can be incredibly motivating.
- This regular feedback helps maintain engagement and momentum, making the learning process more rewarding and effective.

By leveraging these educational tools and platforms, you can create a learning experience tailored to your cognitive style and enrich your personal and professional life.

- The opportunities for learning and development are vast and varied, whether through interactive video tutorials, hands-on simulations, or structured courses with continuous feedback.
- Embracing these tools allows you to take control of your education, turning every learning opportunity into an engaging, fulfilling adventure that plays to your strengths and accommodates your unique learning needs.

8.7 ORGANIZATIONAL TOOLS: FROM DIGITAL CALENDARS TO TASK MANAGERS

In the bustling digital age, managing a myriad of tasks and appointments can often feel like navigating a labyrinth, especially when you're juggling the dynamic demands of ADHD. Fortunately, the design of many digital calendars and task managers keeps you organized and adapts to your unique work-flow, making them indispensable tools in your organizational toolkit. Let's delve into how these tools compare and how they can streamline your day-to-day life.

When selecting the right organizational tool, it's crucial to consider how each platform caters to the nuances of managing ADHD.

Digital calendars like **Google Calendar** and **Microsoft Outlook** provide excellent frameworks for scheduling and reminders.

- **Google Calendar** is exceptionally user-friendly. It offers simple yet effective scheduling tools, easy integration with other Google services, and customizable notification settings that can keep you on track without overwhelming you.
- **Microsoft Outlook**, meanwhile, is robust in handling both calendar management and email organization, making it ideal if you prefer a consolidated tool for both tasks.

On the task management front, applications like **Asana** and **Monday.com** stand out.

- **Asana** allows for detailed task categorization and assignment, which can be incredibly beneficial if you break tasks down into smaller, manageable steps — a common strategy for managing ADHD.
- **Monday.com** offers extensive customization options, from workflows to dashboards, so you can tailor the tool to fit your personal and professional rhythms.

Setting up an effective digital organizer involves more than just choosing the right platform; it's about making it a seamless part of your daily routine.

- Start by syncing your chosen tool across all your devices.

- Synching ensures that your schedule and tasks are up to date regardless of whether you're on your phone, tablet, or computer, providing a consistent organizational experience.
- Share your calendar or tasks with colleagues or family members as needed to aid in collaborative projects or family planning.
- Calendar or task sharing keeps everyone aligned and helps them understand and support your organizational style, which is particularly important when managing ADHD.

Automation within these tools can significantly enhance your productivity. Most digital calendars and task managers offer features like recurring tasks and automatic reminders.

- For instance, setting up a repeat task can be a game-changer for habitual tasks like taking medication or weekly planning.
- Automatic reminders can be an external memory aid, prompting you to start a task or prepare for an appointment. Reminders are crucial when time blindness — a common challenge in ADHD — kicks in.

However, while embracing digital organizational tools, it's vital to consider privacy and security, especially when much of your personal and professional life becomes accessible digitally.

- Always use strong, unique passwords for your accounts and enable two-factor authentication where available to add an extra layer of security.
- Be cautious about how much personal information you share within these apps.

- Familiarize yourself with each platform's privacy settings to control who can see your activities and information.

By leveraging these digital calendars and task managers, you transform them from mere tools to trusted allies in navigating the complexities of daily life with ADHD. They offer more than just reminders and schedules; they provide a structure tailored to enhance your productivity and reduce stress, allowing you to focus more on what truly matters.

As we wrap up this exploration of organizational tools, remember that the goal isn't just to stay organized but to create a system that works for you, enhancing your ability to manage ADHD effectively. These tools are not just about keeping track of your tasks; they're about freeing you to live more fully, confidently, and clearly. Ready to move forward, the next chapter will build on these organizational strategies, introducing advanced planning techniques that cater specifically to the needs of individuals with ADHD, ensuring that every day is well-planned and well-lived.

EMBRACING ADHD: TURNING TRAITS INTO STRENGTHS

Imagine walking into a room where every scattered piece of a jigsaw puzzle finds its place effortlessly, revealing a vibrant, dynamic picture. That's the potential of your life when you learn to embrace and leverage the unique traits of ADHD. Far from being mere obstacles, these traits can be the very superpowers that propel you toward success and fulfillment in various aspects of your life. This chapter will explore how to identify, cultivate, and celebrate these distinctive characteristics, transforming them into tools that enhance your abilities and enrich your personal and professional life.

9.1 IDENTIFYING AND CULTIVATING YOUR ADHD SUPERPOWERS

Recognition of Unique ADHD Traits

You've likely been told countless times about the challenges of ADHD, but what about the strengths that come with it?

- Traits such as hyperfocus, rapid idea generation, resilience in the face of setbacks, and out-of-the-box thinking are not just coping mechanisms; they are genuine strengths that can provide significant advantages.
- The first step in turning these traits into superpowers is recognizing them.
- This step involves a shift in perspective from viewing your ADHD-related behaviors as mere symptoms to seeing them as potential strengths.
- For instance, your natural ability to generate many ideas rapidly is an asset in fields that value innovation and creativity.

Developing Strengths-Based Skills

Once you've identified your ADHD traits, the next step is to actively cultivate them into developed skills.

- This step involves intentional practice and finding suitable environments where these traits can flourish.
- For example, if you excel in rapid idea generation, you might develop this trait further by engaging in activities that require quick thinking, such as brainstorming sessions or creative writing.
- Similarly, if you have a high level of resilience, consider roles or projects that involve navigating challenges or uncertainty, where this trait can be honed and valued.

Practical exercises can also be very effective in developing these skills.

- For instance, try setting aside regular "idea time" to generate as many ideas as possible freely and without judgment.
- Over time, this practice can enhance your ability to think divergently and apply this skill in various contexts.
- Another exercise involves setting progressively challenging goals that require resilience and tracking your progress, which can strengthen this trait.

Utilizing Traits in Daily Life

Integrating your ADHD traits into daily life is crucial for turning them into practical superpowers.

- Find ways to leverage these traits in your projects, work, or social settings.
- For example, if you thrive in dynamic and fast-paced environments, you might take on roles that require rapid problem-solving and adaptability.
- Or, if you have a knack for hyperfocus, you might schedule times during the day when you can work uninterrupted on tasks that benefit from deep concentration.

Furthermore, consider how you use these traits to compensate for areas where you might struggle. For instance, if maintaining organization is a challenge, your ability to think creatively can help you devise unique systems and tools that keep you organized in a way that makes sense. By integrating your ADHD traits into your daily routines and responsibilities, you transform them from abstract concepts into tangible assets that enhance your life and the lives of those around you.

Celebrating ADHD Advantages

Finally, it's important to celebrate and share the successes that arise specifically from your ADHD traits.

- This shift boosts your self-esteem and changes the narrative around ADHD, highlighting it as a source of unique strengths rather than just challenges. Share your achievements with friends, family, or colleagues, explaining how your ADHD traits contributed to your success. Sharing your personal view fosters a positive self-image but also educates others about the value of ADHD traits in a diversity of contexts.
- Additionally, consider contributing your stories and experiences to blogs, forums, or support groups for people with ADHD. Sharing helps build a supportive community and inspires others to view their ADHD more positively.
- By openly celebrating and discussing the advantages of ADHD, you contribute to a broader understanding and appreciation of the condition, fostering a culture that recognizes and values neurodiversity.

Embracing your ADHD traits as superpowers is not just about personal growth; it's about reshaping how ADHD is viewed and experienced. You can turn these traits into powerful tools that propel you toward success and fulfillment by recognizing, developing, utilizing, and celebrating them. This chapter invites you to start seeing your ADHD not as a deficit but as a different set of cognitive tools that, when understood and managed, can lead to remarkable achievements and a profoundly satisfying life.

9.2 CREATIVE PROBLEM SOLVING WITH ADHD

Imagine transforming your whirlwind of thoughts into a powerhouse of innovative solutions. That's the essence of leveraging the natural creativity of an ADHD brain. The tendency to think divergently is a hallmark of ADHD, meaning you can view problems from multiple angles and conjure up solutions that might elude others. This ability can be your greatest asset, whether brainstorming a new marketing campaign at work or figuring out how to reorganize your home in a way that makes sense to your unique brain wiring.

Structured yet flexible thinking processes are the secret to tapping into this creative potential.

Mind mapping and **free writing** techniques are particularly effective as they mimic the ADHD brain's associative thinking pattern.

- **Mind mapping**, for instance, allows you to visually plot out your thoughts using keywords and images in a nonlinear format. This method can be incredibly freeing, as it does not force you to follow a linear path, which can often feel restrictive. Instead, it encourages a free flow of ideas, making it easier to make connections that might take time to make them noticeable.
- **Free writing**, which involves writing continuously without worrying about spelling or grammar, can help bypass the internal editor that stifles creativity. Setting a timer and letting your thoughts spill onto the page might surprise you with the innovative ideas you generate.

However, having many ideas is only one part of the equation.

- Many with ADHD struggle with implementing their innovative ideas, making it the real challenge.
- It requires a shift from divergent to convergent thinking, where you begin to refine and focus your ideas into actionable solutions.
- Facilitate this shift by setting clear criteria for what makes an idea viable and evaluate your brainstormed ideas against the criteria.
- For instance, if you've devised several potential solutions to a work problem, consider the feasibility, impact, and resources needed to implement each idea.
- This process helps hone down your options and prepares you for the next step — taking action.

Implementing creative solutions involves some planning and organization, areas where individuals with ADHD might feel less confident.

- By using tools and strategies that complement your ADHD, such as setting up detailed checklists or using project management software to keep track of tasks, you can effectively bring your creative visions to life.
- It's also helpful to break down larger projects into smaller, manageable steps, a technique that reduces the overwhelm and makes the task seem less daunting.
- Each small step accomplished brings a sense of achievement, keeping your motivation high and driving the project forward.

Case Studies

Let's consider the stories of two individuals with ADHD who have successfully leveraged their creative problem-solving skills.

First, meet Jamie,

- a software developer who used his ability to hyperfocus and his out-of-the-box thinking to create a new app that helps people with ADHD manage their time better.
- Jamie's approach involved using mind mapping to lay out all the app's possible features and then using a prioritization matrix to decide which features were most important.
- His ability to think differently about common problems enabled him to design unique functionalities that made the app particularly helpful for its target users.

Then there's Alex,

- a school teacher with ADHD who transformed her classroom management by implementing creative solutions that catered to her strengths.
- Struggling with traditional methods, she introduced game-based learning and interactive activities that kept her students engaged and allowed her to thrive in an energetic, dynamic environment.
- Her innovative approach improved her students' learning outcomes and brought newfound joy and satisfaction to her teaching.

These stories exemplify how understanding and embracing your unique cognitive style can lead to significant accomplishments.

- By viewing your ADHD not as a barrier but as a different way of thinking, you can unlock a world of possibilities.
- Creative problem-solving is not just about generating ideas. It's about seeing them through to completion, transforming thought into action and chaos into order.
- Whether in your personal life or professional settings, the skills developed through creative problem-solving are invaluable. They enable you to navigate the complexities of life with confidence and creativity.

9.3 THE ROLE OF HYPERFOCUS: HARNESSING INTENSE CONCENTRATION

Hyperfocus is a term that often surfaces in discussions about ADHD, depicting a state where one's focus becomes so narrow and intense that the world around seems to disappear.

- This unique aspect of ADHD is like a double-edged sword; it can lead to remarkable productivity and creativity in certain circumstances, but it can also cause significant disruptions to daily responsibilities if not appropriately managed.
- Understanding hyperfocus starts with recognizing the triggers — those moments or activities that captivate your attention entirely.
- For many, hyperfocus activates during highly interesting or rewarding tasks, such as engaging in creative projects, problem-solving scenarios, or even video games.
- It's like entering a 'flow' state where time and surroundings fade away, leaving you engrossed in the task at hand.

To channel this hyperfocus productively, consider aligning your most attention-absorbing tasks with your peak focus times.

- For instance, if you hyperfocus in the late mornings, schedule your most complex or rewarding tasks during this timeframe.
- This strategic alignment maximizes your natural propensity for deep concentration and helps advance your most important projects.
- Furthermore, setting clear start and end times for these tasks can ensure you stay within focus without causing the detriment of other responsibilities.
- Using timers or alarms can be beneficial here. They gently remind you when to transition your attention to other tasks or take necessary breaks to avoid burnout.

Balancing hyperfocus with everyday responsibilities requires a thoughtful scheduling and task management approach.

- It's easy to let hyperfocus consume your day, leading to neglected duties or uneven productivity.
- To mitigate this, after a period of hyperfocus, take a short break to reset and review your to-do list for the day.
- This break helps reorient your focus toward a broader view of your daily goals and responsibilities.
- Additionally, if hyperfocus frequently pulls you away, breaking your work into shorter segments might be helpful.
- This method not only caters to the natural ebb and flow of attention typical in ADHD but also ensures a more balanced distribution of your focus across various tasks.

Creating an environment conducive to inducing hyperfocus can also enhance your ability to tap into this state when truly needed.

- Start by tailoring your workspace to minimize distractions.
- This tailoring can include wearing noise-canceling headphones to block out external noise or organizing your work area to reduce clutter.
- Specific background music or ambient sounds can also facilitate a hyperfocused state. For many, instrumental music or nature sounds can enhance concentration without the distracting elements of lyrical songs.
- Similarly, the physical setup of your workspace can play a crucial role. Some find that facing a wall rather than a window helps minimize visual distractions, while others prefer a standing desk to keep the body engaged while focusing.

By understanding and strategically managing your hyperfocus, you can transform what others might see as a disruptive symptom of ADHD into a powerful tool for productivity and innovation.

- It's about recognizing when and how to utilize this intense concentration and creating the right conditions to harness it effectively.
- Through thoughtful planning and environment management, hyperfocus can be directed toward tasks that fulfill one's responsibilities and bring a sense of accomplishment and satisfaction, making the most of this unique aspect of ADHD.

9.4 BUILDING RESILIENCE AND FLEXIBILITY

In the ebb and flow of daily life, especially when viewed through the ADHD lens, resilience, and flexibility become more than just traits. They transform into essential skills that empower you to navigate the unpredictable waters of life with poise and confidence.

Cultivating a resilient mindset involves more than just bouncing back from setbacks. It's about forging a path through challenges with an attitude that endures and thrives.

- Cognitive reframing can revolutionize how you perceive and react to the world around you.
- Cognitive reframing involves shifting one's perspective on situations to view them more positively or objectively.
- For instance, instead of viewing a missed deadline as a failure, one could reframe it as an opportunity to reassess one's time management strategies or to improve communication with colleagues about workload expectations.
- This shift in perspective can decrease stress and encourage a more constructive approach to challenges.

Another powerful method for building resilience is rooted in Acceptance and Commitment Therapy (ACT) principles.

- ACT focuses on accepting things as they are, without judgment, while committing to actions that align with your values and goals.
- This approach can be remarkably liberating for someone with ADHD, as it encourages you to accept the

fluctuations in your focus and energy levels as part of your unique neurological makeup rather than as impediments.

- From this place of acceptance, you can commit to actions that genuinely resonate with your personal and professional aspirations, such as pursuing a project that aligns with your passions, even if it requires navigating ADHD-related challenges.
- Regular mindfulness practices can enhance your ability to stay present and focused, further supporting your resilience.

Flexibility in thinking and behavior is equally crucial. It allows you to adapt to changes and challenges without excessive stress or disorientation.

- Try incorporating exercises that challenge your usual thinking or doing things to enhance your cognitive and behavioral flexibility.
- For example, intentionally experiment with new methods or sequences if you have a rigid thinking pattern about accomplishing tasks.
- This pattern change could be as simple as rearranging your morning routine or trying a new approach to a recurring task at work.
- The point is to stretch your cognitive muscles and get comfortable with change, which will make it easier to adapt to unexpected situations.

Learning from setbacks is another key component of building resilience.

- Viewing setbacks as opportunities for growth rather than failures is a powerful reframing that can lead to significant personal development.
- Each challenge or mistake offers valuable insights into what works and what doesn't, which are essential for learning and improvement.
- To foster this mindset, make it a habit to reflect on your experiences, identify lessons learned, and brainstorm how to apply these lessons in the future.
- This reflective practice enhances your problem-solving skills and confidence in handling future challenges.

Numerous resources can guide, inspire, and support you on your journey to building resilience and flexibility.

- Karen Reivich and Andrew Shatté's book *The Resilience Factor* offers practical advice and strategies for developing resilience.
- Workshops and online courses on resilience training can also provide structured learning and interactive experiences that deepen your understanding and skills.
- Websites like **Coursera** or **Udemy** offer expert-taught courses on resilience and flexibility. You can access these courses remotely and conveniently fit them into your schedule.

By actively engaging with these techniques and resources, you not only equip yourself to handle the ups and downs of life with ADHD but also transform these challenges into catalysts for growth and success. Building resilience and flexibility enables you to navigate life's uncertainties confidently, turning potential obstacles into stepping stones for personal and professional development.

9.5 NETWORKING AND BUILDING RELATIONSHIPS WITH ADHD

Networking can often feel like a high-wire act, especially when you're balancing ADHD. The usual advice about networking doesn't always consider the unique challenges you might face, such as forgetfulness or feeling overwhelmed in traditional networking settings like crowded conferences. However, your ADHD also equips you with distinctive traits that can make you a memorable and dynamic networker.

Let's explore tailored strategies that not only accommodate your ADHD but also help you stand out in any professional setting.

- Firstly, understanding your networking style and adapting strategies to fit this style can significantly boost your confidence and effectiveness.
- If large, noisy events make you feel scattered, consider smaller, more intimate gatherings where you can have meaningful conversations.
- Alternatively, online networking platforms can be a great tool, allowing you to connect with new contacts in a controlled environment where you can manage interactions on your terms.
- Preparing in advance can also help mitigate anxiety.
- Before attending an event or meeting, consider what you want to achieve and prepare a few talking points or questions.

- This preparation can help you feel more in control and less likely to be sidetracked by your surroundings.

Using your inherent ADHD traits, such as spontaneity and enthusiasm, can also help you make a lasting impression.

- These traits often lead to vibrant, energetic interactions that make you stand out best.
- Embrace your natural enthusiasm when discussing topics you're passionate about.
- This genuine excitement is infectious and can make conversations more memorable for others.
- Additionally, your spontaneous nature can be a boon in networking settings where adaptability lets you quickly jump into different groups or conversations.
- Just be mindful of balancing this spontaneity with attentiveness to the conversation's flow, ensuring you're responsive to social cues and engage with others' contributions.

Maintaining professional relationships after those initial connections is crucial. Regular follow-ups can keep relationships vibrant and prevent contacts from fading.

- Utilizing tools to manage your contacts can be particularly useful.
- Digital tools like **CRM** (Customer Relationship Management) software or simple scheduling apps can remind you to send follow-up emails or set up meetings.
- These tools can compensate for forgetfulness and help you maintain a consistent presence in your professional circle.
- Sharing an article relevant to a contact's interests or congratulating them on a professional achievement can

keep the relationship warm and show that you value the connection beyond its utility.

Sharing success stories can serve as powerful motivation and provide practical examples of effective networking strategies.

- Consider the story of a graphic designer with ADHD who leveraged her unique blend of creativity and high energy to stand out in networking events.
- She always came prepared with a digital portfolio on her tablet, allowing her to showcase her work dynamically during conversations.
- This portfolio is a great conversation starter and left a visual imprint of her skills with the people she met.
- Her follow-up routine included sending a personalized thank you note and a link to her online portfolio, reinforcing the connection, and ensuring her contacts remembered her long after the event.

These strategies are not just about overcoming the challenges of ADHD; they're about embracing your unique qualities and using them to enhance your networking skills. By preparing strategically, engaging genuinely, and utilizing tools to maintain connections, you can transform networking from a daunting task into an enjoyable and fruitful part of your professional life.

9.6 ADVOCATING FOR ADHD AWARENESS AND UNDERSTANDING IN SOCIETY

Raising awareness about ADHD and dispelling the myths that surround it are crucial steps toward creating a more inclusive and understanding society.

- When you educate others about ADHD, you share information and actively change the narrative about this condition.
- Effective education about ADHD involves clear, accessible explanations and addressing common misconceptions directly.
- For instance, it's important to clarify that ADHD is not just about being hyperactive or distracted; it's a complex neurological condition that affects various aspects of life, from education and work to personal relationships.
- You can use everyday situations or analogies to make these points relatable, such as comparing the ADHD brain to a browser with too many open tabs — both still functioning but with divided attention.

Moreover, tackling the prevalent myths about ADHD head-on can be powerful.

- Many believe that ADHD is a result of poor parenting or a lack of discipline, misconceptions that contribute to stigma and misunderstanding.
- By explaining the scientific research that shows ADHD as a developmental disorder with genetic and biological factors, you can help shift these perceptions.
- Conversations in casual settings or formal presentations provide the platform to challenge these stereotypes and educate those around you.
- Tailoring your communication to your audience — educators, employers, or healthcare professionals — ensures your message is relevant and impactful.

Getting involved in ADHD advocacy groups and initiatives is another effective way to promote understanding and drive change.

- Organizations such as **CHADD** (Children and Adults with Attention-Deficit/Hyperactivity Disorder) or **ADDA** (Attention Deficit Disorder Association) offer resources and community support that can be instrumental in advocacy efforts.
- These groups often organize events, workshops, and seminars where you can contribute your voice and experiences.
- Participating in or organizing such events raises public awareness and builds a supportive community around ADHD.
- By sharing your own stories and the strategies that have helped you, you can inspire others to advocate for themselves or their loved ones, creating a ripple effect that broadens the impact of your efforts.

Creating inclusive environments where individuals with ADHD can thrive is essential to advocacy.

- This effort means working toward accommodations in educational settings, like providing extra time for exams or assignments for students with ADHD or advocating for flexible work arrangements in professional environments, such as the option to work remotely or customize workspace setups to minimize distractions.
- You can advocate for these changes by participating in policy-making discussions or diversity and inclusion committees in your workplace or school.
- By presenting well-researched arguments and concrete examples of how such accommodations can lead to better outcomes, you can influence decision-makers and create environments that recognize and support neurodiversity.

The role of social media in advocating for ADHD awareness is a tool that maximizes reach.

- Platforms like **Facebook**, **X (formerly Twitter)**, and **Instagram** offer powerful tools for sharing information, connecting with others, and mobilizing support.
- By creating or sharing content that educates about ADHD, highlighting personal stories, and promoting ADHD-friendly events or initiatives, you can reach a broad audience quickly and effectively.
- Social media also allows for the formation of online communities where people with ADHD and their families can find support and exchange information.
- Managing a **blog** or a **YouTube** channel dedicated to ADHD can further enhance your impact, providing platforms for more detailed discussions and sharing experiences.

Advocating for ADHD awareness and understanding is part of a more significant movement toward a society that values diversity and inclusion. Every conversation that challenges a stereotype, every event that spreads knowledge, and every post that shares a personal story contributes to this goal. By embracing your role as an advocate, you not only empower yourself and others with ADHD but also enrich the social fabric with greater understanding and compassion.

In wrapping up this chapter, it's clear that advocacy for ADHD awareness is not just about speaking up; it's about engaging, educating, and empowering. As we move forward, let's carry this momentum into exploring the broader implications of ADHD in daily life and society.

KEEPING THE GAME ALIVE

Now you have everything you need to manage your ADHD and find peace amidst the chaos; it's time to pass on your newfound knowledge and show other readers where they can find the same help.

By leaving your honest opinion of this book on Amazon, you'll show other adults with ADHD where they can find the information they're looking for and promote their passion for understanding and managing ADHD.

Thank you for your help. Your role in understanding and managing ADHD is significant, and your knowledge is a vital part of keeping it alive. You're helping me, and the entire ADHD community, to do just that.

Scan the QR code to leave your review.

CONCLUSION

As we end our journey together through this book, I hope you feel a profound sense of empowerment and readiness. We've navigated the complexities of ADHD, transforming challenges into a structured playbook tailored for thriving in every corner of daily life. From mastering time management to enhancing personal and professional relationships, leveraging technology, and simplifying decision-making, our path has been growth and strategic conquest.

This book is a beacon for adults with ADHD. It is a comprehensive guide woven with the latest research, practical tools, and empowering strategies to uplift every facet of life. Whether you're looking to forge deeper connections, excel in your career, or simply manage your day-to-day tasks more efficiently, the insights shared here aim to light your way.

Throughout the chapters, we've explored various strategies and tools, each chosen for its effectiveness and adaptability to the unique needs of living with ADHD. The use of technology as an ally, the emphasis on authentic, applicable solutions, and the incorporation of cutting-edge research make this guide a distinctive and invaluable resource.

I encourage you to take proactive steps toward integrating these strategies into your life. Start with the areas that most resonate with your current needs and challenges. Perhaps it's refining your time management skills or enhancing communication in your relationships. Wherever you choose to begin, allow yourself the space to expand gradually, embracing other strategies for a holistic approach to managing ADHD.

Remember, you are not alone on this journey. Engaging with online and offline communities can provide additional resources, much-needed encouragement, and a sense of belonging. There is immense power in shared experiences and collective wisdom.

I understand that managing ADHD is accompanied by unique challenges, but it's essential to recognize and celebrate your resilience and strength. Let this book be a testament to your journey of self-discovery and growth. Integrating these strategies isn't about overcoming ADHD but about weaving it into the fabric of a balanced and fulfilling life.

I warmly invite you to share your stories of navigating ADHD. Your experiences not only enrich your life but can also inspire and guide others in similar situations. Connect with the community through social media, online forums, or local support groups. Your story can uplift and motivate, fostering a network of support and shared success.

We've equipped ourselves with knowledge and tools to manage and thrive. Keep moving forward, keep adapting, and continue to share your journey. Here's to embracing the full spectrum of life with ADHD, with all its challenges and triumphs. Thank you for allowing me to be a part of your journey.

REFERENCES

Time Management Skills for ADHD Brains: Practical Advice https://www.additudemag.com/time-management-skills-adhd-brain/

ADHD Paralysis and the Best Apps for ADHD 2023 https://www.simcoerehab.ca/2023/02/17/adhd-paralysis-and-the-best-apps-for-adhd-2023/

ADHD Time Blindness: How to Detect It & Regain Control ... https://add.org/adhd-time-blindness/

ADHD and Setting SMART Goals: Learn How to Set Targets https://www.additudemag.com/adhd-and-setting-smart-goals/

Memory Aids and Apps for ADHD, Learning Differences ... https://www.additudemag.com/learning-differences-adhd-memory-aids/

3 to-do list apps that actually work with ADHD https://zapier.com/blog/adhd-to-do-list/

5 Steps To Design Your ADHD-Friendly Workspace For ... https://www.brainzmagazine.com/post/5-steps-to-design-your-adhd-friendly-workspace-for-maximum-productivity

ADHD and Decision Making: Symptoms, Tips, and More https://psychcentral.com/adhd/adults-adhd-tips-to-make-good-decisions

Marriage Communication Tips for Spouses of ADHD Adults https://www.additudemag.com/marriage-communication-tips-adhd-spouses/

How to Show Empathy: Advice for ADHD Brains https://www.additudemag.com/how-to-show-empathy-adhd-friendship/

How to Parent with ADHD: Parenting Skills & Strategies https://www.additudemag.com/parenting-with-adhd-strategies/

ADHD and Anger: Tools for Reducing Family Conflict by ... https://drsharonsaline.com/2020/10/14/adhd-and-anger-tools-for-reducing-family-conflict-by-starting-with-yourself/

ADHD Workplace Accommodations Guide - ADDA https://add.org/adhd-workplace-accommodations-guide/

ADHD Apps: Time Management and Productivity Tools https://www.additudemag.com/adhd-apps-tools-time-management-productivity/

Your Rights to ADHD Accommodations at Work https://www.additudemag.com/adhd-law-americans-with-disabilities-act/

Workplace Issues https://chadd.org/for-adults/workplace-issues/

19 Great Self-Care and Sleep Apps for ADHD Brains https://www.additudemag.com/sleep-app-self-care-adhd/

8 No-Fail Focus Tricks for Adults with ADHD https://www.additudemag.com/how-to-focus-adult-adhd-tips/

Remote Entrepreneurs: 7 Tips for a Distraction-Free Home ... https://www.startupgrind.com/blog/remote-entrepreneurs-7-tips-for-a-distraction-free-home-office/

Passive Noise Isolation vs. Active Noise Cancellation https://us.ultimateears.com/blogs/music/passive-noise-isolation-vs-active-noise-cancellation

6 Essential Mindfulness Practices To Help With 6 Common ... https://www.adhdcentre.co.uk/6-essential-mindfulness-practices-to-help-with-6-common-adhd-symptoms/

10 Strategies For Managing ADHD & Impulsivity In Adults https://laconciergepsychologist.com/blog/10-strategies-managing-adhd-impulsivity/

Rejection Sensitive Dysphoria (RSD): Symptoms & Treatment https://my.clevelandclinic.org/health/diseases/24099-rejection-sensitive-dysphoria-rsd

The Best Apps For ADHD In 2024: A Guide https://www.forbes.com/health/mind/apps-for-adhd/

32 of the Best Ways to Get Organized When You Have ADHD https://psychcentral.com/adhd/the-best-ways-to-get-organized-when-you-have-adhd

Marie Kondo for ADHD https://www.anitarobertson.com/new-blog/2019/2/4/konmarie-method-for-adhd

38 Apps and Add-Ons That Transformed My Productivity https://www.additudemag.com/best-productivity-apps-adhd-adults/

Bullet Journaling to Help ADHD Minds in Quarantine - ADDitude https://www.additudemag.com/bullet-journaling-adhd-quarantine/#:

Reduced Symptoms of Inattention after Dietary Omega-3 ... https://www.nature.com/articles/npp201573

The Exercise Prescription for ADHD https://chadd.org/wp-content/uploads/2018/06/ATTN_06_12_Exercise.pdf

Guide for a Better Sleep When You Have ADHD https://www.donefirst.com/blog/guide-for-a-better-sleep-when-you-have-adhd

Nutrition in the Management of ADHD: A Review of Recent ... https://www.ncbi.nlm.nih.gov/pmc/articles/PMC10444659/

Time Management Skills for ADHD Brains: Practical Advice https://www.additudemag.com/time-management-skills-adhd-brain/

The relation between procrastination and symptoms ... https://www.ncbi.nlm.nih.gov/pmc/articles/PMC6878228/

Physical exercise in attention deficit hyperactivity disorder https://www.ncbi.nlm.nih.gov/pmc/articles/PMC6945516/

Best Mental Health Apps for ADHD https://www.additudemag.com/slideshows/best-mental-health-apps-for-adhd-headspace-talkspace-better-help/

DSM-5 Criteria for ADHD: How Is Adult ADHD Evaluated? https://add.org/adhd-dsm-5-criteria/

ADHD Medications: How They Work Side Effects https://my.clevelandclinic.org/health/treatments/11766-adhd-medication

Checklist for Choosing the Best Therapist for ADHD https://overcomewithus.com/therapy-for-adhd/checklist-for-choosing-the-best-therapist-for-adhd

ADHD and Complementary Health Approaches: What the ... https://www.nccih.nih.gov/health/providers/digest/adhd-and-complementary-health-approaches-science

38 Apps and Add-Ons That Transformed My Productivity https://www.additudemag.com/best-productivity-apps-adhd-adults/

Gamified Interventions for ADHD: Wearables, Digital ... https://www.additudemag.com/digital-therapeutics-adhd-lumosity-meta-quest-endeavorrx/

Using Communication Technology to Improve Relationships https://www.psychologytoday.com/intl/blog/conscious-communication/201808/using-communication-technology-improve-relationships

6 Online ADHD Management Tools for Adults - ADDA https://add.org/adhd-tools-for-adults/

Creativity in ADHD: Goal-Directed Motivation and Domain ... https://www.ncbi.nlm.nih.gov/pmc/articles/PMC7543022/

The Ultimate ADHD Career Advancement Guide [2021] https://adhdcollective.com/adhd-career-advancement-guide/

ADHD support groups: Benefits, options, and more https://www.medicalnewstoday.com/articles/adhd-support-groups

Born This Way: Personal Stories of Life with ADHD https://www.additudemag.com/adhd-personal-stories-real-life-people-living-with-adhd/

Student Academic Resource Center. (2020). **Eisenhower Matrix Fillable,** University of Central Florida. Retrieved from https://academicsuccess.ucf.edu/sarc/wp-content/uploads/sites/31/2020/12/Eisenhower-Matrix-Fillable.pdf